*"Regardless of what an_____
perfect system of executi____*

Perhaps bluff, outspoken Harry Allen knew better than
anyone when he said that. For he held a public service
job that no man is ever likely to hold again. He was
Britain's last hangman.

Among his 82 "culprits," as he liked to call them,
were such high-profile murderers as James Hanratty,
the A6 rapist-killer, Victor Terry, the Worthing bank
robber, cop-killer Guenther Podola, and Peter Manuel,
Scotland's worst-ever serial killer.

As an assistant executioner Harry participated in the
hanging of 53 "culprits," who included 19-year-old
Derek Bentley, who has since been pardoned, and five
Nazi prisoners-of-war. As chief executioner he was
responsible for 29 hangings, including the last man
to be hanged in Britain before the abolition of capital
punishment.

In this absorbing chronicle of his life, his opinions
and his executions, Harry emerges as a free-speaking
no-nonsense Lancastrian who firmly believed that
murderers should pay the price for their crimes on the
scaffold.

Here's how the hangman was trained, how he worked,
how he treated the condemned men on the gallows, and
how he stood up to his critics, the abolitionists. Here
is a book that brings a new dimension to the capital
punishment debate – focusing on a man who knew more
about it than anyone else in Britain.

•

STEWART McLAUGHLIN is a prison officer based
at Wandsworth Prison, London. He has also written
Execution Suite (2004) and *Wandsworth Prison – A
History* (2001).

HARRY ALLEN:
BRITAIN'S LAST
HANGMAN

Stewart McLaughlin

Published by True Crime Library,
the paperback division of Magazine Design
and Publishing Ltd.
PO Box 735, London SE26 5NQ, UK

An imprint of True Crime Library
© 2008 True Crime Library
All rights reserved

Cover design by Ben James
Designed and typeset by Declan Meehan
Printed and bound in Great Britain by
CPI Cox & Wyman, Reading, Berkshire

ISBN 978-1-874358-42-8

For Doris Allen

CONTENTS

CONTENTS

CHAPTER 1

HOW TO BECOME A HANGMAN

Unlike most schoolboys of his time, 11-year-old Harry Allen didn't dream of becoming a railway train driver or a ship's captain. His dream was focused when he read newspaper accounts of one of the most sensational murder trials of the 20th century.

After that Harry had a yearning ambition. He wanted to be a hangman.

There was little likelihood in those days that capital punishment would be abolished. There was no reason for young Harry to think that the job would ever become redundant. The future for executioners looked as bright as the future for coal miners. Eventually he achieved his ambition. But it was one no other Briton is likely to achieve – for he became Britain's last hangman.

Harry Bernard Allen was born on November 5th, 1911, to James and Emma Allen, of 50 Braithwell Street, Denaby, Yorkshire. He had two older sisters, Christine and Vera, and two brothers, James and Albert, would later join them.

There are some memories that the family had been in Scotland, but Harry's earliest thoughts really stemmed from his upbringing in 2 Oakenclough, Limehurst, Lancashire.

When he was a schoolboy the First World War was in full carnage, and his father, serving with the Manchester Regiment, was fighting in the trenches.

With dad away from home and three females in the family, women, especially his mum, to whom he was very close, inevitably influenced the early period of his life. He remembered his schooldays in Ashton under Lyme, but he didn't much like school until a Mrs. Marmer began teaching him when he was about six years old. When the war ended in 1918 his dad, one of the lucky survivors, came home to resume his place at the head of the household, and life became more orderly and disciplined. Now the children were expected to do small chores around the house, a sure indication that James Allen had brought some military organisation back with him from the Western Front.

When Harry's father caught him smoking, the cigarettes were confiscated and he got his backside whacked. That wasn't an uncommon punishment for such a misdemeanour in those days. But there was more to James Allen than just a firm disciplinarian. He also had a good singing voice, good enough for public performances in Limehurst.

So, popular songs of the day, many of them songs of the war, were frequently heard filling the house at Oakenclough when concert time was drawing near, and together with Charlie Chaplin silent movies they formed the background of young Harry's leisure hours when he wasn't struggling with his school work. But perhaps his subconscious mind was already at work on his future career, for one indelible memory stands out among all others in his schoolboy years. That was the trial for murder and subsequent hanging, in 1923, of Edith Thompson.

Harry was 12 when Edith Jessie Thompson, who was more than twice his age, was arrested. She had been married for about seven years when tragedy engulfed her, her husband, and her lover. For almost the whole of those seven years she and Percy Thompson had lived the ordinary uneventful lives of a normal husband and wife, in a suburban semi in Ilford, Essex.

Edith, though, was ahead of her time. She had a job in central London, commuted every day, and she earned more than her husband. In the early 1920s, even given the gender revolution that followed the First World War, that set her apart from most other women in Britain. Something else set her even further apart from other married women – she had a lover. By the standards of her day, that made her very daring indeed.

Childless, she worked as a bookkeeper and manageress of a central London millinery business, where she earned the very considerable sum of £6 a week, plus bonuses. Percy Thompson's salary as a shipping clerk didn't nearly match that, but their combined salaries meant that they could live in exceeding comfort, with regular visits to theatres and restaurants.

But the Thompsons were not well suited. She had a vividly romantic imagination, and buried herself in cheap novelettes where the denouement was a passionate embrace and a lingering kiss. He, by contrast, had no imagination at all, and his only reading was confined to the shipping news and the racing papers.

As she wrapped herself up in her latest storybook, Edith saw herself as a heroine, often in some distant corner of the world, falling in love with a handsome Oriental prince who carried her off to a dreamy paradise where he was able to satisfy her ardent, passionate nature. When she woke up from this secret, sensual world, she was in her Ilford semi, alongside her shipping clerk husband.

One day in the spring of 1921 Edith visited her mother's house and was introduced to a handsome young man who was dating her younger sister. His name was Freddie Bywaters, and although he was a simple laundry steward on the P & O liner *Morea*, Edith transformed him in her imagination to a worldwide traveller, a dashing naval officer who could sweep her off her feet, from Ilford to the seven seas.

In short, Edith fell in love. It was soon pretty clear too that Freddie was much more interested in the married sister than the unmarried one. When the Thompsons went on holiday that year to Shanklin in the Isle of Wight, Freddie went too. Somehow, while Percy wasn't looking, she got Freddie into her bed and plunged into a passion that she had only been able to dream about all her married life. All her cheap novelettes came true at once as the woman of 28 and the youth of 19 became clandestine lovers.

Percy always made Bywaters welcome at the Thompson home, because at that time he had no suspicions about his wife's torrid affair. Bywaters actually stayed in the

Ilford semi for some weeks as a paying guest. When he went off on his travels Edith bridged the gap of their parting by a passionate correspondence in which she fantasised about life with Freddie and without Percy. From her novelettes she extrapolated plots to poison her husband, and in his letters Freddie Bywaters seemed to go along with them.

Like Edith, Freddie had lost his head. In a piece of foolishness that must surely have been his crowning mistake, he kept all Edith's letters. On almost every page of those burning epistles she referred to abortive attempts to cause her husband's death so that she could be united with her illicit lover. And the strangest thing of all was that all those murderous ideas probably only existed in her mind – they had absolutely no substance in reality.

One evening in October, 1922, Percy and Edith, who were outwardly at least on the happiest terms with each other, went to a theatre in the West End. On the way home they were walking from the station the last few hundred yards to their house when a figure emerged silently from the shadows and stabbed Percy Thompson.

A passer-by heard Edith suddenly scream out, "Oh, whatever shall I do? My husband has fallen and cut his head!"

The whole case against Edith when she was put on trial for her husband's murder turned upon those few seconds. Did she know that the figure in the shadows was her lover? Did she know he was going to kill Percy? Did she recognise the assassin and instinctively try to shield him, even though she was overcome with horror? Or did she have no idea at all?

These questions were pondered over for years after the event, and they swirled around in the mind of young Harry Allen as he read the morning papers. The most likely interpretation of the tragedy was that Edith fantasised about her husband being dead, making her a free woman, but would never in reality have been a willing party to his death, and when it happened she profoundly wished it had not. She almost certainly had no idea what was in Bywaters' mind, or that he would be lurking in the shadows that night.

At any rate, a doctor was called, and by the flickering light of a match he pronounced the crumpled body on the pavement as having died of a haemorrhage. Not until the body was taken to the mortuary was it discovered that Percy Thompson had actually been murdered – stabbed three times so savagely that he must have died at once.

That point established, the police swiftly interrogated the hysterical widow. She said she was entirely unable to throw any light on how her husband was killed; she hadn't the faintest idea whose hand came out of the night so suddenly to assassinate him as he walked at her side.

But a heavy knife, still stained with blood, was found in a nearby street drain. It belonged to Freddie Bywaters.

He was arrested, and in his cabin on the *Morea* they found Edith's extraordinary fantasising letters. So she was arrested too, and they faced trial for conspiring together to murder Percy Thompson.

During their five days in the dock at the Old Bailey her letters were read out to a wide-eyed audience. But the judge, Mr. Justice Shearman, wouldn't hear that there was anything romantic about Edith and Freddie's love. It was, he said, an ordinary charge of a wife and an adulterer murdering a husband. The word "adulterer" had a stinging Edwardian ring to it; so too did the judge's declared view that it was wrong that a wife's love for another man should be seen to be romantic, while her love for her husband should be scorned.

The truth was that Edith's letters were pure fantasy, and if there was a hint of wistfulness about them that didn't link her with Bywaters' stabbing of her husband. And her trial was bound to be prejudiced because she faced a court full of people still immersed in pre-First World War social concepts: married women didn't work; they didn't earn more than their husbands; they didn't have lovers – perish the thought! – and some people probably even thought they shouldn't read books.

After the judge's summing-up, the jury took two and a quarter hours to bring in guilty verdicts against the two defendants. Stunned, Edith screamed from the dock: "I am not guilty – oh, God, I am not guilty." But already the judge had on his black cap.

Now the British public accomplished one of those remarkable *voltes-face* for which it is renowned. Up until this point Edith Thompson had been universally execrated. She was publicly accused of being worse than an adulteress – her letters, according to *vox populi*, proved that she had set out to murder her husband, and she undoubtedly urged on her lover to kill him. No sooner was sentence of death passed, however, than a wave of protest swept through the country. At first no one had imagined that a woman was going to be hanged – that hadn't happened for 15 years, and modern life was altogether different now. It was argued of course that you could hardly spare the woman and hang the man.

The authorities took no notice of this. They briefed public executioner John Ellis, who was nearing the end of his 23-year stint as Britain's chief executioner. "The question of hanging a woman who did not actually commit the murder, and who was thought by many people to be innocent, troubled me for hours," Ellis said. "In the end I decided it was my duty to obey instructions. I guessed the general public would regard me as a morbid, depraved monster, and I wasn't long left in any doubt about that. The anonymous letter fiends were about to have a ball with me over Edith Thompson."

Edith, meanwhile, was in Holloway Prison. "I am not going to die," she often said to the wardress whose melancholy duty it was to keep her company. "My reprieve will come. But, oh! This dreadful waiting."

Even as Ellis was checking into the prison on January 8th, 1923 – the day before the execution and the same day that Freddie Bywaters was hanged at Pentonville

Prison by another hangman – she was confidently writing to friends, discussing such things as books she had read and her mother's birthday. When her mother, father, sister and brother turned up to visit her that same day she implanted in their minds the idea that she would be saved, chatting quite cheerfully to them, and parted from them without even bidding the customary goodbyes.

But that night Edith fainted, and the prison governor advised Ellis that there might be trouble on the scaffold. Already she was a pitiable sight. She had crumpled physically, and appeared to be in a state of semi-collapse.

John Ellis had to do some sums before he hanged Edith Thompson. The heavier a person is, the shorter the hangman makes the drop, so that a light person has a long drop. For Ellis, the maximum dropping distance was 10 feet. The total length of the drop under the trap-doors was 12 feet. The hangman fixes the length of the drop after weighing up the condemned person, taking into account their height, weight and any other factors he feels should be included in the equation.

The decision is a critical one, because if he underestimates the drop the victim will not die at once of a broken neck, which is the object of modern hanging methods, but will be strangled. If on the other hand he overestimates, the resultant jerk can pull off the victim's head.

At 5 ft 8 in Edith Thompson was quite tall for a woman. She had actually gained 11 lb in weight in the three weeks she had been under sentence of death, pushing her weight up to 9 stone 4 lb. Ellis decided upon a drop of 6 ft 10 in, which, he said, was less than the drop he would have given a man of the same size, and 10 inches less than the Home Office regulations suggested for the height and weight. Asked why, he said: "Because we are dealing with a woman – a matter of physical difference that the Home Office grades don't recognise."

Next day Ellis and his two assistants rose at 6.30.

Ellis took a peep at Edith in the condemned cell. She was still asleep. A little later he took another peep and was relieved to see that she was now dressed, seemingly bright and cheerful and laughing at the jokes of the two wardresses who were there to keep her mind off what was coming at nine o'clock.

Ellis and his two assistants busied themselves about the execution chamber. Its only item of furniture, besides the grim crossbeam, a coil of rope and the lever beside the trap-doors, was a chair. This was not for the doomed woman, but it was needed for the chaplain, who had made a point of asking for it, as he suffered from fits of dizziness.

At 8.55 Ellis went to meet the prison governor. There were several other prison officers present. They were silent as the governor held his watch in his hand, measuring out the last fast-flying seconds of Edith's life.

Ellis recalled: "At three minutes to nine we all heard an eerie sound. It was a low moan from the condemned cell. It startled me, perhaps, more than the others. The officers were much more used to Mrs. Thompson's nerves giving way periodically, and were aware, because they had been told about it in the last few minutes, that this was happening now. It was something of a shock to me, because my last glimpse of her had been so reassuring. Afterwards I heard she had nibbled a piece of buttered toast and an apple after she was dressed, and had remained quite composed and in good spirits until quite near the execution hour."

Ellis was very shocked, and, he said, they were about to view a scene "that will never fade from my memory." When he walked to the condemned cell at one minute to nine he found Edith in a state of complete collapse – she had lost all control of herself. The chaplain and the two wardresses were bravely trying to console her. Unable to stand, she was lifted to her feet by the wardresses, while her cries and semi-demented body movements began to have an effect even on her executioner. He pinioned her hands behind her back, working as fast as he could.

Edith's head slumped – she had fainted again. Mercifully she was never to emerge from her unconsciousness. Ellis told his assistants: "Strap her skirt around her ankles." To the warders standing by he rapped: "When that's done, all of you carry her to the scaffold."

Looking as if she were already dead, she was carried to the death chamber by four men. Ellis recalled: "I put the white cap on her head and face and slipped the noose over all. It was agonising just to see her being held up by the four men, her bound feet on the trap-doors. Her head had fallen forward on her chest, and she was completely oblivious to what was going on. Without giving a moment for anything further to happen, I sprang the lever. One flick of my wrist and Mrs. Thompson disappeared from view.

"She died instantaneously and painlessly. I saw her afterwards, when I helped the matron in her unpleasant task of putting her body in her coffin, and her face was calm and composed, as if she were peacefully asleep."

Nine years later John Ellis featured in his last execution – his own. He was 58 when, imbued with memories he had failed to obliterate, he cut his throat and bled to death.

At the age of 12 Harry Allen read the story of Edith Thompson and her execution and, notwithstanding its inherent judicial cruelty, resolved to become an executioner. He doesn't seem to have shown much interest in any other capital crimes while at school. Perhaps that was because his headmaster, Mr. Cooper, swishing his cane, was indoctrinating him into the painful business of corporal punishment.

For as a schoolboy Harry developed a reputation for practical joking. One piece of mischief he recalled was played on a local Limehurst man known by everyone as "Mr. Don't." His job was tapping on people's windows and doors to get them out of bed in the morning. That may seem bizarre today, but this was a time when watches and clocks were not so readily available as they are these days. "Mr. Don't" acquired his nickname as result of telling people, "Don't be late" on his morning rounds.

"Mr. Don't" also did a bit of totting – buying and selling rags and bones. One day he left his horse and cart near Harry's school and went off to have a liquid lunch. While he was gone Harry and his friends unhitched the horse and tied it up inside the school playground. When "Mr. Don't" re-appeared he was bewildered, and when he found out who was responsible he went ballistic.

The law in Limehurst was Police Constable Swarbrick, a large man with a big moustache who meted out summary justice with no right of appeal. Children caught by the constable making mischief would have their ears clipped or would feel his boot on their backsides. Harry's only encounter with PC Swarbrick came about when a local sweetshop owner named Broadbent complained about children constantly staring through his shop window. The constable's hand reached out and caught Harry's ear. After that, the youngster kept a better eye out for the law.

Harry was a good sportsman, playing football and cricket, and a moderately good swimmer. Much like other kids of his age in those times, he also played marbles and collected cigarette cards. For the uninitiated, cigarette cards ran in series of 48 or 50 and depicted sporting heroes, historical figures, buildings, ships, cars, aeroplanes, or whatever, and were popular collectors' items, especially among small boys whose parents smoked – there was one free card in every pack. Face to face with pictures of such heroes, inventions and events, young Harry was seemingly unimpressed. He didn't want to play cricket for England, or football for Manchester United, ride speedway, or travel into darkest Africa. He wanted simply to be a hangman.

He would for certain not have made a scholar. Although his handwriting and arithmetic were judged to be of very high standard, they were the only things that counted at elementary school, as it used to be called in those days, and the opportunities for higher education were limited. So Harry left school at 14, and because in the 1920s there existed no career structure for a 14-year-old to train as a hangman, he had to start thinking of something else to do in the interim.

That something else was an apprenticeship in engineering for the firm of Joshua Heaps in Ashton under Lyme. It wasn't what he wanted. Being holed up in a factory, with the smell of grease and heavy machinery, didn't appeal to a sporting lad. He wanted fresh air and open country, together with freedom to roam and make at least some of his own decisions. The ideal job was to become a driver.

Horses were still much in evidence for transportation, but this was the age of the internal combustion engine. Livery stables were being converted to garages with petrol services, and young men were enthralled by the prospects of travelling at 20 miles an hour. A Manchester company called Simpson's took Harry on, and the call of the open road beckoned.

His main work was to make deliveries in a Model T Ford. Once, he made a trip to Liverpool on roads that were narrow and unfamiliar to him. He did the round trip faster than any of the company's other drivers, earning the plaudits of his manager. There was still no official driving test and no driving licences – you sat at the wheel, took off, and learned as you went.

By the time he was 21, Harry was ready to become a lorry driver. Because the job now took him away from home, he centred his life on lodgings in Manchester and travelled all over the country, stopping overnight in places as far away as London. Evidently, though, Manchester was the chief attraction, for the people with whom he lodged had a pretty daughter named Marjorie, and Harry had set his cap at her. They were married in 1933.

These were hard times. The great depression had settled heavily over Britain. The northern unemployed marched from Jarrow to London demanding jobs from a government that had no idea how to provide them. Civil war raged in Spain as General Franco, one of the continent's fascist dictators, stifled popular opinion, and the spectre of another world war loomed as Hitler and

Mussolini strutted and threatened. On the home front the abdication crisis had the monarchy tottering.

Harry still yearned to become an executioner, and there is more than one theory about what actually made him step forward at about this time to apply for a job as assistant executioner. His son Brian says he had become friendly with Thomas Pierrepoint, one of the family of hangmen whose doyen was Albert Pierrepoint. Harry may have met Thomas Pierrepoint during his long-distance travels as a lorry driver. Brian Allen remembers Tom as a kindly grandfather figure, and it seems certain that Harry discussed hanging with Tom.

Another theory is that having made deliveries to Manchester Prison, Harry was attracted by the idea of becoming a prison officer, but took a hangman's job instead. This seems unlikely, since the recruiting process for prison officers was entirely different. Somewhere in the back of his mind must have been the story he had read as a boy of the unfortunate Edith Thompson and, together with the chance of travel, overnight stays and pay, plus his belief in the value of doing a professional job, he plumped to become a hangman.

You didn't just "become a hangman," however. The process of recruiting executioners was not one of people responding to advertisements. The Prison Commission trained recruits only if an absolute need arose. At the time of Harry's application the Home Office was receiving between five and 10 letters a week from prospective hangmen. If all had been successful, that would have made anything from 250 to 500 a year, while there were jobs for five or six at the most. This was a much-sought-after job, and only the best were likely to get it.

The much-discussed impending war became a reality on September 3rd, 1939, putting most of the country's domestic plans for the future on indefinite hold. What then for the future of hangmen and for capital punishment? With the threat of a breakdown of ordered life it was reasoned that capital punishment might have to be increased. Subsequent records show that this view was the right one – there was in fact an increase in the use of capital punishment during the war years.

Harry Allen's application, which can be dated at either 1939 or 1940, got him an interview with the governor of Manchester Prison. He was no stranger to the prison gates because of his deliveries. It would have been a matter of form for the prison medical officer to be present at the interview so as to be certain of the motives of the potential candidate.

He was certainly lucky even to get an interview. Letters from people wanting to become executioners were generally read and sifted. Pre-printed acknowledgement replies were sent out and any applicants who had divulged dubious reasons to become executioners had their names excluded from going any further in the selection process. No doubt there were plenty of avenging angel types and applicants with an unhealthy wish to participate in the death of someone.

Applications that got through this process would be kept on file, but if nothing had happened after a year these letters too were filed away for good. While some applicants wrote only once and perhaps waited a year for further action, others wrote almost yearly until they were accepted for an interview.

Harry passed the Manchester interview with no problems and next received a letter from the governor of Pentonville Prison in London inviting him to attend a week's training in August, 1940, with the object of becoming an assistant executioner.

It was perhaps one of the very worst periods in the capital's long history to be starting a course on anything. As he stepped off the train Harry was confronted with the results of the Blitz. Air raid sirens wailing every night heralded the next enemy air attack, searchlights flared in the sky, barrage balloons dotted the horizon. There were sandbags around the shops and rubble from the damage caused by the bombing in the streets. Altogether it was a grim welcome for the new recruit.

At the time of Harry's arrival there, Pentonville Prison had already been emptied of ordinary prisoners for the duration of the war but was still held available for prisoners under sentence of death. The gallows was housed on the second landing on A Wing with the condemned cells next to it. It was here that the trainee executioners received their lessons.

So it was that in August, 1940, Harry reported to governor's office. With him were three other potential executioner candidates – Steve Wade from Doncaster, Harry Critchell from Pimlico, London, and Harry Kirk from Catford, London.

The governor sat behind his big desk and outlined the training week. They would be under the tutorship of Mr. Pugh, foreman of the works, and they would have written and practical tests on their last day, Friday. They were reminded that they were now apprentices on government business and bound by the Official Secrets Act, so anything they learned or did was not to be reported to anyone outside.

When Harry's course began the trainees had just missed the execution of Udham Singh at the prison on July 31st. The hangman in that case was Stanley Cross from Fulham, assisted by Albert Pierrepoint. Cross and Albert Pierrepoint had trained together at Pentonville as long ago as 1932.

Before executions began at Pentonville they were held at Newgate Prison. Then in 1902 the Newgate execution suite was transferred to Pentonville and housed in a shed off the prison's B Wing. The execution process was modernised in 1929-30 with a new gallows, together with two condemned cells in A Wing to ensure a more efficient operation.

The first day of the theory instruction for Harry Allen was an explanation of the administration system that brings a prisoner to be executed. This would be followed by more theory explaining how hanging breaks the neck, and there would be an explanation of the Table of Drops to assist in the calculation of how long a drop should be. The modern method of hanging moved away from straight strangulation to neck-breaking in the 19th century.

In his memoirs *The Hangman's Tale*, executioner Syd Dernley recalls how his instructor, eight years after Harry Allen's training, told him about neck-breaking: "Hanging is efficient, clean and above all very quick. As you can see, the distance the man has to be moved between his cell and the gallows is short and once the trap-doors are opened and he goes down, he's killed instantly by having his neck broken.

"For any of you who is anatomically minded, it parts the second and third vertebrae. The fact that it is so fast is a kindness to the man who has to go and to the people who have to be present at the execution. It also means that so far as the hangmen are concerned, they have to know exactly what they're doing and they have to get it right first time. There is no margin for error – remember that."

Harry was taught how the apparatus of crossbeam, rope and trap-doors worked together. The trainees made sketches and took notes.

Next, the theory had to be put to the test with a visit to the gallows. Tools needed were chalk to mark the spot where the doomed man stood, a measuring rod for the drop, a white hood to put over his head, and wrist and ankle straps. The gallows' operation was tested with a bag filled with sand, weighed on scales, replecating the condemned prisoner, and a sewn ball and neck for a head.

The instructor showed how the arm strap, fastened by a double buckle arrangement, and the ankle strap were used. The ankle strap was demonstrated at speed – it was always the last job for the hangman before he pushed the lever.

Having familiarised themselves with the equipment and how to use it, the trainees then practised again and again, swapping roles. The emphasis was on speed and efficiency, and to achieve that it really was a case of practice makes perfect.

Although Pentonville was the centre of training for budding executioners, it did not keep execution equipment in store. This was housed at Wandsworth

Prison, in south London, which meant that whenever an execution was scheduled, boxes of kit were dispatched from Wandsworth to Pentonville. As a wartime measure, some execution equipment was also held at Bristol and Manchester prisons.

In the week-long training, Harry's final test on Friday included a written exam and a practice hanging in front of the prison governor, who at this time was Mr. L. C. Ball. Harry and the other trainees all passed, but before their names were placed on the list of assistant executioners, they first had to witness an actual execution for themselves.

For Harry, a letter from Bedford Prison dated November 20th, 1940, confirmed the date of execution of William Henry Cooper on the 26th of that month. Harry was to be second assistant at the hanging. The letter from the prison governor, with all its official stiffness, (but perhaps not with its rather wonky syntax), was standard procedure:

Dear Sir,

With reference to my letter of the 15th inst. and your provisional acceptance to undertake the duties of Second Assistant executioner in the execution of the above named convict at this prison, I have to inform you that the High Sheriff has fixed Tuesday next the 26th inst. at 9 a.m. as the date and time fixed for the carrying out of the sentence. I therefore have to request that you will report to this prison on the 25th. inst not later than 4 p.m. Prepared to carry out your duties the following morning.

A return railway warrant to Bedford is enclosed, which please return if your services are not required. The date is final as far as the high sheriff is concerned, but is, of course, subject to possible interference by the Secretary of State. Should the arrangements be altered you will be notified immediately so far as you may be concerned.

The condemned man, William Cooper, a farm worker, was convicted at Cambridge for the murder of John Harrison, an elderly farmer, on October 17th. Mr. Harrison had sacked Cooper, but the real motive for murder was probably to steal the wages Mr. Harrison was known to be carrying on a Friday morning. Cooper got it all wrong, however, for when he attacked his old boss Mr. Harrison had already paid his workers the previous day.

Harry arrived at Bedford Prison on the afternoon of November 25th. He met Thomas and Albert Pierrepoint, who were to conduct the execution, and Steve Wade, who was also there to observe. He would have noticed that Bedford was not an ideal place to hang a man – its gallows was then probably the only one remaining in the UK located in a separate blockhouse detached from the main prison wing. This caused an obvious delay in the execution proceedings, painful for the condemned man and for the officials.

The morning after Harry's arrival at the prison, William Cooper went to the gallows with a drop of 8 ft 1 in. Afterwards Harry wrote his first notes in the execution diary he had decided to keep: "Very good and clean job carried out at Bedford by Mr Thomas W. Pierrepoint. The culprit [Cooper] had to be carried to the scaffold owing to faintness and loss of courage but not until the same morning. He played dominoes and cards until 10 p.m. the preceding night with the warders."

Now that he had been a witness, styled "second assistant" but really required to do nothing but observe, and presumably having shown no damaging emotion, he was now qualified to be a genuine assistant. Later on in his career this must have caused some pain to Home Office bureaucrats, because there would be two Harry Allens on the assistant executioners' list.

Syd Dernley explained how he discovered this when one day he got into a London taxi with Albert Pierrepoint. They had come down from Manchester and were on their way to a hanging, via Barney Finnegan's Irish pub, a favourite watering hole of the chief executioner. By this time our Harry Allen had become a long-established assistant executioner, and he was high up on the list to become a chief executioner.

Dernley remembered: "On the way he [Pierrepoint]

told me that the other men on the job were to be my old mate Harry Allen and another man, from Manchester, also called Harry Allen. They were not related; it was just a strange coincidence that there were two men of the same name on the list and they both happened to be on this job."

In fact, Dernley's "old mate Harry Allen" was a Birmingham man, and the two Allens were often distinguished by being referred to as the Birmingham Allen and the Manchester Allen. But the name of the Birmingham Allen wasn't really Harry at all – he appeared on the Home Office list under his real name, Herbert Allen.

Later that day, says Dernley, "We met the two Harry Allens at Wandsworth. The Manchester Harry Allen seemed a cheerful type, if a little flamboyant; I could scarcely believe the bow tie! He was friendly enough, in a condescending way that announced that he was the senior assistant and we were mere newcomers."

All that, though, was in the future. The first job Harry was asked to perform was to assist in the hanging of Clifford Holmes at Strangeways on February 11th, 1941. Holmes had come home on leave from the army to discover his wife Irene was having an affair, so he murdered her. Harry noted in his execution diary: "Very good job carried out at Strangeways by Mr. Thomas W. Pierrepoint. Very cheerful [this, presumably, refers to Holmes]. Time taken, 14 seconds."

Next was Henry White, lying in the condemned cell at Durham Prison. White murdered his girl friend, Emily Wardle, by cutting her throat in front of a witness in Bertram Street, South Shields. Harry's execution diary note, dated March 6th, 1941, read: "Very quiet culprit, walked without aid and stood correct. The chief executioner was Thomas William Pierrepoint and the job was carried out at H.M. Prison Durham."

It was some months before Harry was back in action again. He was at Strangeways assisting Tom Pierrepoint in the execution of John Smith on September 4th, 1941. Smith had also murdered his girl friend, Margaret

Knight, because he thought she had finished with him.

Harry's execution diary note reads on this occasion: "First job carried out by A. Pierrepoint as senior executioner, very nice and good performance all through." This was not entirely accurate, as Albert Pierrepoint officiated as an executioner for his first time at Pentonville Prison on October 31st when, assisted by Steve Wade, he hanged a London gangster, Antonio Mancini.

In a Home Office list of executioners dated May, 1941, Harry Allen's name and that of assistant executioner Alexander Riley are asterisked. The footnote reads: "The service of these two assistants are not to be called upon at present, due to circumstances arising from the war."

What this meant was that Harry was on essential war service, although precisely what that was is somewhat mysterious. His "day job" was long-distance lorry-driving, and there was a shortage of drivers because most of them were already in the armed forces. Long-distance lorry-driving would certainly have been classified as essential war work, because of the need to distribute foodstuffs and vital supplies around a beleaguered country.

But was his war service more glamorous than just that? The question arises and is intriguing because Harry's son Brian remembers that many years after the war, when his father was landlord of the Junction Hotel at Whitefield, a man came into the bar and recognised Harry. They had met apparently during the war, and they spent all evening and the following morning reminiscing. Brian recalls the name Major Boddington, and his involvement as an organiser of the Dutch resistance during the German occupation of the Netherlands. Your author's research into the files of the Special Operations Executive reveals an officer named Boddington, but his involvement was with the French resistance.

The list with the request not to employ the two assistants may not have gone round to all prison governors, for both men were employed at executions within a short time. Alexander Riley was back in business from August, 1943, and Harry was employed on a few executions after May, 1941. Although prison governors were the actual employers of execution assistants, they obtained the names from a list provided by the Prison Commissioners. The Prison Commission had to re-locate during the war, and it therefore may have been an administrative error that caused Harry to be summoned to assist at the 1942 execution of David Williams at Liverpool Prison. As it happened, he turned down the request, probably making it known that he was not available because of his war work, and Steve Wade took the assignment, assisting Tom Pierrepoint on March 25th. Harry did not return to capital punishment until the end of the war in 1945, when, after contacting the Home Office, he was re-appointed an assistant hangman.

CHAPTER 2

FIVE NAZIS ON THE SCAFFOLD

Whatever lay behind the mystery of Harry's "war work," he was back in business bright and breezy as ever at the war's end, ready to resume his official duties. During his absence his fellow-trainee executioners had risen up the pecking order, with Steve Wade now closely behind Albert Pierrepoint. Albert was the nephew of the chief executioner Thomas Pierrepoint, and was himself well on the way to becoming chief executioner.

The first job offered to Harry, less than a fortnight after his reinstatement, was to assist at the execution of Ernest Bramham, convicted for the murder of Eleanor Hammerton, a widow in her 80s. The day was to end differently from almost all other execution days. After Harry had rigged the gallows for testing and checked all the equipment, a message arrived from the prison governor – there would be no execution, Bramham had been reprieved.

Prior to every execution there was a statutory medical inquiry, and as the doctors examined Bramham they came to the conclusion that he was insane. The Home Secretary was informed and a reprieve was ordered. This type of 11th-hour reprieve was very unusual, and more typical of Hollywood movies than real life. Interestingly, I remember a case at Pentonville where the documentation of the execution had been written up with all the details apart from the execution itself. Then came a reprieve, and the execution details had to be left blank.

The next job was also to be very different from routine executions. This time there would be five men on the scaffold with nooses around their necks.

They were all German prisoners-of-war and they were found guilty of killing another POW they believed to be an informer.

In September, 1944, the German POWs had all been incarcerated at a camp in Devizes, Wiltshire, where they had been working on an elaborate escape plan. The ringleader was Erich Pallme Koenig, a fervent Nazi. But it all came to nothing, for in December the plan was discovered. The result was that a number of prisoners were swiftly transferred to Comrie in Perthshire – not exactly Colditz, but where, if nothing else, escape would be that much harder.

Did someone betray the escape plan? If so, who was it? Koenig and his unofficial camp committee were convinced that it was Sergeant-Major Wolfgang Rostberg, a regular soldier in the German army, as distinct from a wartime conscript. Unlike many of the other POWs, Rostberg was in his mid-30s and not a Nazi. He could speak English and was employed as the camp's interpreter, which meant that he was in constant contact with the British authorities.

Soon after the prisoners arrived at Comrie, Rostberg was dragged from his bed and given a summary "trial" by a group of Nazi POWs thirsting for revenge. He was found guilty of betraying the escape attempt. He was beaten until he was unrecognisable and then hanged in a washroom building. His body was found next day, December 23rd.

The local police and military called in Scotland Yard, but detectives met a wall of silence erected by the Nazi SS code of silence. No one would say anything. The murder inquiry was returned to the army and in January, 1945, Captain John Wheatley went to the camp to conduct an investigation.

Slowly the events of that December night became clearer and names were identified. But there were further dark threats to non-Nazi prisoners, and evidence given was sometimes retracted.

In March, 1945, with the end of the war only a few weeks away, the POW camp was given a new commandant. He was Colonel Archibald Wilson, a former chief constable. Determined to eradicate the slackness in the camp, he enforced a regime of discipline, particularly to curb the behaviour of fanatical Nazis. Nazi salutes were banned, along with all other outward displays of Nazism. In addition, Colonel Wilson was determined to have the killers of Wolfgang Rostberg brought to justice. He was reinforced in these measures when camp security passed from British soldiers to Polish nationals, who had no fondness for the Germans.

The news of Hitler's suicide was met with disbelief by the Nazi POWs, and when it was followed up almost immediately by the news of Germany's surrender there was an immediate impact on their morale and the course of the investigation. The pace of the inquiry quickened and as the VE Day celebrations swept across Europe, eight men found themselves facing a murder charge. They were sent to a military court martial in London.

They were brought to trial at No. 8 Kensington Gardens, one of those mysteriously secret addresses that were dotted around central London during the war. This one was known as The London Cage, and it was believed to be the office of a secret military intelligence organisation.

The eight prisoners were Erich Koenig, the escape organiser, Heinz Brueling, Joachim Goltz, Rolf Herzig, Hans Klein, Josef Mertens, Herbert Wunderlich and Kurt Zeuhisdorff. Their predicament was completely absurd. They were accused of killing a man they believed had foiled their escape from a camp where, in a matter of months, they would have been freed anyway, and all for a cause that was collapsing around them while the crime was being committed.

The trial revealed the extent of the influence of fanatical Nazis within the camp, and the hold they had over the less committed prisoners. Witnesses gave testimony against most of the accused, and described how Rostberg was brutally beaten before he was hanged.

Hans Klein and Herbert Wunderlich were found not guilty. The remaining six were found guilty and sentenced to death. On July 10th, 1945, they were transferred to Pentonville Prison.

Under a proviso of the Geneva Convention, the government was required not to carry out the sentence for three months, while further inquiries into the procedure were conducted. This turned out to be a lucky break for Rolf Herzig who, during the waiting period, had his death sentence commuted to life imprisonment.

Appointed assistant executioner to Albert Pierrepoint, Harry Allen reported to Pentonville on October 5th, 1945. There he met up with the other assistant, Steve Wade, his old colleague from training days in 1940. The prison was a grim, hollow shell of a place. Although it had been closed for ordinary use during the war, it was still used to execute prisoners convicted of capital crimes.

The executions of the German prisoners began at 9 a.m. on October 6th. They were executed singly, and their bodies were not left at the end of the rope for the usual one-hour period. They were hanged in the order of Goltz, Brueling, Mertens, Zeuhisdorff and Koenig. The last man, the ringleader, was defiant to the end, shouting "Alles für Deutschland" as the trap-door opened beneath his feet.

Interestingly, Harry Allen had a tenuous connection to the executed Nazis when his younger brother Albert was posted to Kensington Palace Gardens to guard them before the court martial. One of the German prisoners mended a watch for Albert, which made Albert more sympathetic to their plight. The brothers Allen may well have had different views as a result of being both keeper and executioner of their charges.

Harry was an assistant executioner for 14 years. Except for two cases, the killers he helped to hang were not for the most part involved in crimes that hit the headlines. The first of the two high-profile cases was unique because it centred upon the first-ever death in Britain of a have-a-go man. His name was Alec de Antiquis, and after the shot that killed him on a London street nothing was ever quite the same.

The murder not only ended the life of an innocent man, it also provided an unhappy close to the career of a legendary courtroom figure. It gave the first big chance to a detective who was later to become famous. And it set the pattern for a wave of violence that would later stretch the resources of Britain's forces to their limit.

"This is the start of a new era in crime," a Scotland Yard official said at the time. He was right. The "new" crime was armed robbery. We may be accustomed to it today, but in 1947 the thought of a single pistol being aimed in anger was enough to spark off newspaper stories of "Chicago-style violence."

The streets of London were safe. Passers-by could be relied upon to tackle fleeing raiders without fear of ending up as target practice. Scotland Yard even encouraged bystanders to "have a go" at bandits. But behind this official complacency, a new breed of criminal was emerging – shiftless, brutal young thugs with a contempt for "old-fashioned coppers" and law-abiding citizens alike.

They had grown up during the war, often without proper parental control, and drifted quickly into the get-rich-quick spivvery that was a feature of the otherwise austere life of the 1940s.

One of them was 23-year-old Charles Henry Jenkins, who prided himself on being the "King of Borstal." Despite that royal title, Jenkins was just a small-time sneak thief with a taste for violence.

On April 23rd, 1947, he left prison for the last time, determined to start afresh. Not as a petty housebreaker, but as a gun-toting bandit. Almost before the jail door clanged behind him, he got his gang together. There was Bill Walsh, known only as "Joe," and a 20-year-old tearaway named Christopher James Geraghty.

They wasted no time in inaugurating their new careers. Armed with pistols, they raided a jeweller's shop in the Bayswater area of London and got away with loot worth £5,000.

Then things went wrong. Instead of the expected

share-out, the youngsters got nothing. When they reassembled there was no Bill Walsh. He had double-crossed them and run off with the takings.

It was a bitter lesson for Jenkins. For his next exploit he vowed he would only recruit "mates" – people he trusted.

They had no time to lose. Both Jenkins and Geraghty were broke. On the night of April 27th, Jenkins, Geraghty and a 17-year-old youth named Terence Rolt broke into F. Dyke and Co's gunsmiths' shop in Union Street, Southwark. They spent several hours choosing weapons and ammunition. In their ignorance they pocketed sample cartridges that had long since deteriorated.

On the morning of Tuesday, April 29th, the three armed youths met outside Whitechapel tube station and travelled to Goodge Street to case the jewellers' shops. Eventually they settled on Jay's, a corner shop in Charlotte Street – an untidy road of shops and restaurants at the northern end of Soho.

But they couldn't agree on the value of the display, and because it wasn't safe to hang around outside the shop, they huddled in a café, popping out every now and then to take a fresh look at the window. At 2 p.m. Jenkins had had enough of waiting. "Right," he said. "Let's do it, then."

Like everything else about them, their planning was hapless and disorganised. They had no getaway vehicle, so Jenkins and Rolt went off to steal a black Vauxhall from nearby Whitfield Street. From all the cars available, they managed to choose a dud.

Rolt was appointed the driver, but his knowledge of getaway driving was so dim that he switched off the engine and accompanied the others into the shop. All three wore handkerchief masks and carried guns.

Ernest Stock, the manager, looked up to find himself staring into the barrels of the levelled revolvers.

"This is a stick-up!" snarled one of the bandits, reaching for a tray of rings. Mr. Stock didn't scare so easily. He leapt forward, and one of the men smashed a revolver down on his head. As he fell, a bullet, fired in panic by one of the raiders, zipped across the shop. Mr. Stock's 17-year-old assistant hurled a stool at one of the bandits and jumped for the burglar alarm.

The clanging confused the raiders. One threw his gun at the assistant. He didn't know it at that moment, but that was all it was good for. He had loaded it with so many different sorts of ammunition that it couldn't be fired. Then they fled, clutching a few items, back to the car.

But the Vauxhall wouldn't start. The ignition wheezed and clattered, refusing to fire. Rolt was still struggling with the starter when a van drew into the kerb, blocking their way.

"Out!" yelled one of the bandits. They piled out of the car into the street, threatening the growing crowd with their guns. Among the passers-by at this moment, on his way for a drink at the Fitzroy Tavern in Charlotte Street, was the chief executioner, Albert Pierrepoint. At this moment too Alec de Antiquis appeared on his motorbike. He was 35, a family man with six children, struggling to build up a small motorcycle repair business in south London.

He would not have called himself a hero, but in that split-second he summed up the situation and recognised his duty. British bandits, as everyone knew, only used their guns to frighten people, and stopped short at actually pulling the trigger. He decided to "have a go."

The people on the pavement saw him swing his motorbike in front of the bandits, shouting and waving an arm. Then there was a sharp crack, and he fell. Bystanders rushed to his aid. As the bandits disappeared down the street – dropping a silver cake stand on the way – he coughed, "They shot me...get them."

De Antiquis died on the way to hospital. He had been shot in the head at point-blank range.

Later that day the legendary pathologist Sir Bernard Spilsbury performed a post-mortem. His commanding physical presence, and his expert medical evidence, had dominated British courtrooms for decades. Now, however, he was in decline, a sick and unsure old man. Puzzled and confused, he probed for the exit wound of the bullet, unaware that it had dropped from the dead man's head on to the floor. This was his last case – eight months later he committed suicide.

But for Chief Inspector Robert Fabian it would be the beginning of a spectacular career. Solving the case was his first major triumph. He took charge of the investigation almost by accident. His superior was away, and Fabian was alerted in the middle of lunch. Without bothering to wait for dessert or coffee, he dashed out to establish his murder headquarters at Tottenham Court Road police station.

Fabian knew that as long as the killers remained at large, every trigger-happy ruffian would be tempted to follow their example. His feelings were echoed at the highest level. Sir Ronald Howe, head of the C.I.D., decided to mobilise all his men in the manhunt. "This crime is an outrage!" he declared.

For the first time a Scotland Yard chief sent an open invitation to the underworld – rapidly growing restless under the build-up of police pressure – to turn in the wanted men. "The best way to finish this," was the gist of Fabian's message, "is to finger the killers for us."

But the bandits were young and callow amateurs, as unknown to the underworld as they were to the police.

On the third day of the manhunt, a taxi-driver gave the Yard men their first lead. He said a man tried to jump into his cab near Charlotte Street on the afternoon of the murder. But the cabbie already had a passenger, and the man made off into a large building nearby. Fabian's men searched the building, and in an empty office on the top floor they found a pair of gloves, a cap, a handkerchief knotted into a mask, and a raincoat.

The coat was cheap and well worn, of a kind made in thousands. Fabian had the seams unstitched. Under the armpit, in faded red ink, was a manufacturer's number: 7,800. Raincoat manufacturers all over Britain were contacted, and the makers were traced to Leeds.

In April, 1947, a legacy of the Second World War was

that clothes were still rationed and could only be bought by handing in coupons, which bore the buyer's name. Starting from the point of the raincoat's discovery, Fabian's men fanned out to the shops to which the Leeds raincoats had been distributed.

Hundreds of coupons were sifted. One, for a fawn raincoat, made Fabian pause. It bore the name of George Vernon, and the police chief remembered that Vernon was married to the sister of a vicious thug named Charles Henry Jenkins. When Fabian called at the Vernon home, Mrs. Vernon told him that her husband had lost the raincoat a few weeks earlier. Jenkins was released from prison only six days before the Soho murder. Could he have borrowed the raincoat?

Brought in to the murder headquarters, Jenkins cockily provided an alibi for April 29th, the day of the murder. Fabian had no alternative but to let him go.

Meanwhile, two new clues turned up. An eight-year-old boy found a revolver on the Thames foreshore at Wapping. It was a .320 loaded with five live cartridges and a spent case. Three of the rounds had misfired. Top ballistics expert Robert Churchill identified it as the weapon that killed Alec de Antiquis.

A few days later another boy found another gun – a .455 Bulldog revolver loaded with four live rounds and one empty case. Again, Churchill examined the weapon. It was the one that fired the shot into the wall of Jay's jewellery shop.

Even before he saw the two guns, one thought persistently nagged Chief Inspector Fabian. That was the similarity between the Soho hold-up and the armed robbery at Bayswater six days earlier, the day Jenkins quit prison.

Fabian now took a fresh line, ordering his men to keep an eye on receivers of stolen property. Within a few days a Southend fence was picked up. He gave the name of the man who sold him some of the loot from the Bayswater job. It was Bill Walsh, the man who had double-crossed Jenkins.

Walsh was interrogated for hours. Finally he gave the

names of his two accomplices in the Bayswater robbery – Jenkins and Christopher James Geraghty.

Two hours later Jenkins was back in front of Fabian. This time his alibi fell apart at the seams.

"Where were you on the 29th?" Fabian demanded.

"I know exactly where I was," Jenkins snarled, "but I'm not talking yet!"

Jenkins admitted borrowing the telltale raincoat from his brother-in-law, but claimed that he lent it to Walsh. This was a crude attempt at implicating Walsh in the Charlotte Street shooting, but it didn't work.

Jenkins didn't know that Walsh had already confessed to Fabian that he cheated his partners in the Bayswater robbery by running off with the loot. The confession cost Walsh five years in jail – but it was enough to clear him of any involvement in the murder of Alec de Antiquis.

Now it was the turn of Geraghty. First, however, Fabian organised a spot of amateur dramatics. As Geraghty was escorted into Tottenham Court Road police station, Fabian made sure he saw Jenkins being marched in the opposite direction. Geraghty appeared shaken.

To begin with, Geraghty tried to act the tough guy. Gradually his assurance sagged. It didn't take too long to squeeze out the name of the third member of the Charlotte Street gang – Terence Rolt. "It was his panic that caused all the trouble," sneered Geraghty.

Hours later, tired and bewildered, Geraghty revealed the name of the killer of Alec de Antiquis. "It was me," he said. "I didn't mean to kill him. I fired at him to frighten him."

Geraghty's revolver fired for the last time at the Old Bailey, where all three stood trial for murder. Asked to demonstrate how quickly he could fire the weapon, Robert Churchill pointed it dramatically at the ceiling and squeezed the trigger four times in rapid succession. The clicks were heard right across the hushed courtroom.

The jury found all three men guilty. Because of his

youth, Rolt was sentenced to be detained during His Majesty's pleasure. Geraghty and Jenkins were sent back to Pentonville to be hanged on September 19th by Albert Pierrepoint, a bystander at the murder scene, assisted by Harry Allen and Harry Critchell.

One thing still puzzled people: why had the name "George Vernon" on the clothing coupon immediately led Fabian to think of the Jenkins family? Jenkins was only a small-time villain. There seemed no reason why his name should have stuck so firmly in Fabian's mind.

The sadly ironic answer was provided a few months later when at a London ceremony, Alec de Antiquis was posthumously awarded the Binney Medal for bravery in helping the police. The medal is named after Captain Ralph Binney, who was knocked down and killed by a smash-and-grab raider's car near London Bridge.

It happened only three years before the murder of Alec de Antiquis, and the reason why the name Vernon meant so much to Chief Inspector Fabian was that one of the criminals in the smash-and-grab raid was called Jenkins. The coincidence didn't end there. He was the brother of Charles Henry Jenkins.

In a sense Geraghty and Jenkins might have considered themselves unlucky, for even as early as 1947 whether or not someone condemned to death was actually executed was becoming something of a lottery. In April, 1948, the Commons debated a Criminal Justice Bill that included a five-year suspension of the death penalty. With this in place, the Home Secretary reprieved all those sentenced to death. When the Bill reached the Lords the suspension of the death penalty was deleted and the Bill became law in June. The law also removed corporal punishment from the courts, although it remained a prison punishment. With the resumption of capital punishment, it would still be a few months before the due process of law would end with an actual execution.

One of those who was sentenced to death and was due to be hanged with Harry as the assistant was the notorious child-killer John Thomas Straffen, who suffered from mental health issues from a young age. He was released from a mental health institution in 1951 and only a few months later he killed two children. At his trial he was adjudged insane and was sent to Broadmoor. He escaped, and although he was only free for an afternoon he killed another child, Linda Bowyer, before he was re-captured. For this murder he was tried at Winchester, found guilty and sentenced to death.

The question arose, if he was mad in the first place and belonged in Broadmoor, how had that situation been changed simply by his escape and his killing a third time? An objective observer might have reasoned that this was all a reflection of the turmoil the law of murder was in during the post-war years. In the event, it was wisely suggested that as Straffen had already been adjudged mad, he couldn't hang. Harry Allen, already appointed assistant executioner for Straffen's date with the scaffold, was advised at the last moment by the Prison Commissioners that his services wouldn't be required because the sentence had been "respited." The child-killer was sent back to Broadmoor, where he spent the rest of his life.

The second high-profile murder case involving Harry in his years as an assistant was another one that revealed the confusing state of the law. It was a case that reverberated down the years until recent times, and it was the only case on record in which Harry himself objected to being involved in hanging the accused man, and made his view felt to the authorities.

It began when a call was picked up by Croydon Police on Sunday evening, November 2nd, 1952, that two men had been seen trying to break into the Barlow and Parker confectionery factory building. They were subsequently identified as Christopher Craig, aged 16, and Derek Bentley, aged 19. Craig had a fascination for guns and had one with him on that fateful evening.

Detective Constable Frederick Fairfax and several police constables climbed to the roof of the building where the two men had been spotted. Bentley was arrested and held by DC Fairfax, who had removed a knife and a knuckle-duster from his prisoner. When it was reported that gunshots were being heard, more police rushed to the rooftop scene. At one point DC Fairfax was hit by a bullet and faltered back, taking Bentley with him.

Much was subsequently to be made of a call from Bentley: "Let him have it." This may have been an invitation to Craig to fire; it might have been, as was later contended, a plea to give up his gun; or it might never have been said, if Craig was to be believed. At any rate, PC Sidney Miles was moving between chimney stacks when a shot from Craig's gun struck him in the head, killing him instantly.

Sidney Miles was a married man and had been a police officer for many years. He was a keen darts player and one of his colleagues remembers seeing the dead body with darts sticking out of his pocket. The police on the roof withdrew, taking with them the body of Sidney Miles, and also Derek Bentley, who was in a confused and upset state.

DC Fairfax and other officers returned to the rooftop, but this time they were armed. After an exchange of threats, Craig fell from the roof of the building through a greenhouse roof. He was taken to hospital.

On Monday, November 3rd, Derek Bentley was bought before Croydon magistrates, charged with murder, a charge that also applied to Christopher Craig.

Derek Bentley came from a close working-class family background. He was born in 1933 in Blackfriars, just south of the Thames, the sole survivor of twins. He suffered a head injury when he was four, had to be dug out of the family air raid shelter when he was seven after his grandmother and elder sister were killed, and was again injured when a V1 flying bomb hit his home in 1944.

When the war was over the family settled in Norbury, south London, where Derek got involved in petty crime, and usually got caught. He was sent to Kingswood approved school, near Bristol, where his IQ was discovered to be 66, with a reading age equivalent to a four-and-a-half-year-old. Additionally he suffered from epilepsy, which ruled him out of National Service.

Bentley met Christopher Craig at the end of 1951. Craig's father was a former First World War army officer, commanded a Home Guard unit in the second, and was a senior official in a bank.

Bentley's father never took to Christopher Craig, whom he saw as a bad influence on his son. Nor did he like Craig's elder brother, Niven Scott Craig, who the following year would be sentenced to 12 years for armed robbery. Despite his efforts to keep his son away from young Craig, the pair met on the evening of November 2nd, just a couple of hours before they got involved in the rooftop gun battle.

When Craig and Bentley were on remand in Brixton Prison both were assessed as fit to stand trial. It was their misfortune, perhaps that when they came to the Old Bailey on Thursday, December 9th, 1952, the presiding judge was Rayner Goddard, the Lord Chief Justice, who had established a reputation as a judge with a remarkable lack of sympathy for the accused. He made numerous interruptions during the evidence, the vast majority of them showing bias towards the prosecution. The impression he gave was that he had already decided on the case, possibly because the victim was a policeman. That, effectively, was not balanced off against Bentley's pathetically poor mental state. Although Bentley was the older of the two he had the mind of a child, and it was clear which of the two had been the leader.

The case against Christopher Craig was fairly damning, but it was not so clear against Derek Bentley. He was under arrest when the fatal shooting occurred and the shout "Let him have it" was denied by Craig. A policeman who was not called to give evidence would have said that he did not hear the shout. During his summing-up, Lord Goddard put on the knuckleduster that was taken from Bentley, a gesture fit to appeal to the emotions of the jury.

On December 11th the jury returned verdicts of guilty of murder against both youths. For Bentley there was a recommendation for mercy. Bentley was sentenced to death, while Craig, who could not be hanged because of his youth, was given a life sentence. In fact, he was released 10 years later.

Bentley was taken to Wandsworth Prison, London, where he was given a quick medical before changing out of his civilian clothes into prison-issue clothing, especially made to prevent any part of it being used to assist in a suicide attempt.

The condemned cell, one of a pair, was three single cells knocked into one, with large windows covered by mesh. The entrance from the outside was up a metal staircase through a lobby area, one cell's width, that looked like a cloakroom. Turning right through a door led to the condemned cell. Turning left, behind the coat hooks and green shutters, were the gallows.

The Bentley family returned home that night in a state of shock. They now had the fight of their lives on their hands. They visited Derek, and found him keeping a cheerful view of things. The visiting room for prisoners under sentence of death prevented any physical contact – the area was the size of two cells, connected by a ticket office window with fine mesh around the glass to allow sound to pass through.

On January 13th, 1953, Bentley's appeal was dismissed, and campaigns began to spare his life. But the clock was ticking on remorselessly, and by a letter dated January 19th Harry Allen was asked to assist at the execution, arranged for January 28th. Meanwhile, the Home Secretary, Sir David Maxwell Fyfe, decided not to interfere with the course of the law, and in Parliament the Speaker of the Commons refused to allow a debate on the subject.

Brian Allen, Harry's son, was about the same age as Derek Bentley at the time, and he vividly remembers his father's views on the execution. Harry was distinctly unimpressed with the law that asked him to hang a 19-

year-old with the mind of a child. He tried to contact a Home Office official and was given excuses for not being put through, but he kept on calling until an official came to the phone. Harry told him that the job he did would be betrayed if people like Derek Bentley were to go to the gallows. The Home Office official's response was not recorded, but Harry's action indicated that he had some distaste for this case. It also indicated that the law-enforcement authorities were muddle-headed over capital punishment, because if there were a case for it, that case was now going to be seriously undermined by the hanging of a youth like Bentley and the imprisoning of a youth like Craig.

Further on in his career Harry recalled the execution of Bentley and said: "He's the only one I wish I had never hanged. It was wrong that he was executed for what his friend did."

But after his retirement he appeared to have a serious change of heart about Bentley, for he wrote an article for the *News of the World* in which he said:

"Much fuss was made about the fact that the life of Craig, who fired the fatal shot, was spared, while Bentley went to the gallows.

"But these two young men armed themselves with deadly weapons to go out stealing. And as a result a brave policeman died. I reckon they both deserved to hang. Craig's free today and should count himself lucky."

A large crowd assembled outside Wandsworth Prison on the morning of January 28th. The previous day a single notice was displayed, informing the public that Derek Bentley would be executed next day. At the time the execution took place, the crowd fell silent. When, finally, the statutory notice was posted informing the public that the execution had taken place at 9 a.m., the crowd surged forward and began throwing whatever they had to hand at the notice. The glass frame holding the announcement was smashed and the police had to use physical force to restrain the demonstrators.

The Bentley family never gave up their campaign to

establish Derek's innocence on the murder charge. As a result of their efforts, a Royal Pardon in respect of the sentence was granted in July, 1993. Five years later, in July 1998, the conviction for murder was quashed. Derek Bentley emerges as an innocent man, wrongly convicted, wrongly sentenced.

•

It was perhaps because of cases like this that half-way through his 25-year career as a hangman Harry Allen began to ask questions about himself and the job. He was never able to give convincing answers to people who asked him why he got involved in the first place. He would talk about it with a kind of passivity, as though he had been reluctantly forced to accept the inevitable.

"I wrote to the Home Office in 1939. They offered me a job as assistant executioner. Unfortunately I accepted. My wife was completely against it but at that time I had no choice but to take it on."

It is difficult to see why there was no choice. It could not have been a question of money – at that time assistant executioners were paid under £3 for each job. Pressed about this, Harry was rather vague, and talked about a desire for security against the uncertain background of the 1930s.

Was he looking for the security of some official position, then? He had some civil servant-like characteristics – a taste for careful circumlocution, a mild air of self-importance that set him apart in a crowd. He liked formal suits with waistcoats, bow ties, and affected a traditional bowler hat.

Once he mused: "I never enjoyed executing people. No more than a vet does when he puts a sick animal to sleep. But just like the vet, I try to make death as quick and as painless as possible. And we're very fast."

His personality in mid-life was a mixture of heaviness and saloon bar joviality. He could have been the town clerk of some northern community or perhaps the leading light of a chamber of commerce. He also looked slightly out of date – the kind of character Priestley might have included in *The Good Companions*.

He was already married to Marjorie, his first wife, by the time he applied to the Home Office for the job, but she failed to influence his decision to accept the offer when it came in 1940. "I didn't think it was up to her. Yes, I'm a Catholic, but I didn't discuss it with the clergy either. I didn't think it came within their particular rights of judgment."

Years later he went public on the fate of the Moors murderers, Ian Brady and Myra Hindley. He believed, he said, that Britain could have been saved years of anger, anguish and expense if the authorities had given him just 15 seconds in which to hang the notorious pair of child killers.

Brady and Hindley cheated the noose by six months. When they committed their dreadful catalogue of crimes Britain still had the death penalty. But by the time they came to trial the following year it had been abolished.

That, said Harry, was the biggest mistake the country could ever have made. "They should both have been executed," he said. "Look at all the trouble they've caused in prison. We could have saved a lot of money by hanging them."

He believed that, faced with the scaffold, Hindley would have made a full confession to the murders of Keith Bennett and Pauline Reade – a confession that was only wrung out of her after 20 years behind bars. That was a view supported by many of the police officers involved in the original investigation, but for a different reason.

With the death penalty hanging over their heads, murderers would try to escape the noose by pleading insanity. To help convince the judge and jury that they were insane, they would confess to all their crimes, on the basis of the more the madder.

Harry's view was rejected by Chief Superintendent Arthur Benfield, who headed the murder inquiry. He said: "There was no question of capital punishment. Brady and Hindley were not fools. Why should they admit any more crimes? If they had done so, there would have been no question of release in the future."

But Harry claimed that Brady and Hindley knew the government was phasing out hanging while they were indulging themselves in their orgy of murder. "I'm sure that encouraged them," he said. "I bet they rejoiced in their cells when the anti-hanging Bill was passed before their trial."

Disappointed by the post-1965 escalation of violence, he had become very pro-hanging, claiming that he was supported by the statistics. In 1965 there were nearly 400 homicides in Britain. In 1986, when Harry was 75, there were 662. "I blame the well-meaning do-gooders for the mess that society's in today," he said. "As a nation, we've gone soft."

History has shown that there have been some good hangmen, and some very bad ones. Harry Allen was undoubtedly a good hangman – one who did the job efficiently, who didn't bodge things, who was never put on report by a testy prison governor upset at the way an execution had gone badly in the few minutes that the condemned man has to go from his cell to the scaffold. In more than 80 executions, that was a very good record.

One essential ingredient of that excellent career was that he never forgot his training instructor's advice about the importance of getting the drop exactly right. Years later he gave an interview in which he dwelt heavily on that vital aspect of the hangman's job.

"My routine was always the same," he said. "As soon as a prisoner was condemned to death by the courts I would receive a letter saying my services would be required, and another informing me of the exact date and time of the execution.

"I'd contact my assistant and arrange to go with him to the prison where the condemned man was being held, on the day before the execution. We would arrive at the prison after lunch. I always wore a suit and a bowler hat with a wide range of multi-coloured bow ties, so that anyone demonstrating outside the jail would assume I was a doctor or a lawyer. I didn't want to get involved in any aggro with the anti-hanging brigade.

"After meeting the prison governor, my assistant and I would observe the prisoner while he was exercising. We would always stay out of sight to spare his feelings. The prison doctor would already have given me up-to-date details of the prisoner's height and weight.

"I had to know the prisoner's exact weight, and the significance of it is the amount of rope required to hang him. These details are worked out to one-thousandth of an inch. They have to be that precise because one of my predecessors, James Berry, was haunted by technical errors. Mr. Berry, a former policeman, was appointed chief executioner in 1883. When he was summoned to hang John Lee, a footman convicted of murdering his wealthy woman employer, Berry tested the trap-door successfully.

"But when he pulled the lever at the actual execution the doors failed to open. Lee was removed for a few minutes while Berry again tested the apparatus. It worked perfectly.

"Everyone returned to their appointed positions and Berry again pulled the lever. Nothing happened. A third attempt produced the same negative result. The Under Sheriff then consulted the Home Office, and the end result was that Lee was reprieved, and his death sentence commuted to life imprisonment. Presumably it was believed that some sort of divine intervention saved him.

"This was almost true. Years later it was revealed that the reason why the trap-door mechanism failed was because the chaplain was inadvertently standing on a warped board, which jammed the apparatus.

"In 1892 there was another unhappy incident. Berry had a prolonged argument with a prison doctor about the length of drop for the execution of John Conway in Liverpool. Berry thought the recommended drop was too long and said: 'If it pulls his head off, I'll never hang another.'

"Berry's worst fears were confirmed. He resigned, became a fervent abolitionist, and turned to drink."

Berry was succeeded by a Bolton hairdresser named John Billington; after him came Henry Pierrepoint and then John Ellis took on the job. His "customers" included Dr. Crippen and Sir Roger Casement. The succession continued until in 1956 Harry Allen took over from Albert Pierrepoint.

Harry went on: "John Ellis also proved unequal to the demanding task. After hanging a number of notorious murderers, he suffered acute depression and eventually committed suicide. Knowing these stories about my predecessors, I became a stickler for detail. We would have a dummy run the night before, using a sack of sand and a mannequin's head.

"The rehearsal takes all the stretch out of the rope and ensures that the drop is exact.

"If it was an 8 a.m. hanging I would get up at 7 and give the equipment a final test. At about 7.55 I'd go to the door of the condemned cell to meet the prison governor, engineer, and doctor. The chaplain and two prison officers would be inside the condemned cell with the prisoner.

"At the first stroke of 8 o'clock we would go in. I'd immediately pinion the prisoner's hands behind his back with a belt made of doeskin fastened with a buckle. Then we would lead him some ten paces to the scaffold outside the cell and stand him in position above the trap-door. All the time the chaplain would be following, reading out a funeral service.

"I would place the noose, about a thumb's width thick, around the prisoner's neck with the knot underneath one of his ears. This would break the neck at the fourth vertebrae and sever the adjacent nerve.

"While I placed a white hood, like a pillow case, over the prisoner's head, my assistant would strap his knees together around the knees and ankles. This is to stop any post-mortem nervous twitching.

"I'd then step to one side, three feet from the condemned man, and pull the lever. The trap-door, 4ft wide and 3ft across, opens. Death is instantaneous.

"In just over the time it takes to read a five-line sentence in a newspaper a man can be escorted from his cell to the scaffold and hanged. From the moment we entered a murderer's cell to the moment he falls through the trap is about 11 seconds.

"There's no opportunity for last-minute speeches, songs or jokes from the prisoner. Even he doesn't realise just how quick it will be. Perhaps he is still waiting for a last-minute reprieve. Who knows? Ninety per cent manage to say, 'God forgive me,' or 'I'm sorry, mum.' That's about all they have time for.

"We would leave the body hanging there until the doctor went below to certify death. Then we would haul it back with a pulley and gently lower it down. There's never any mark on the corpse.

"My assistant would undress the body and we'd put it in the coffin, and our job was over. After breakfast I always used to return home, have a bath and go to bed. I slept like a baby for the next eight hours. I've never been bothered with dreams or nightmares."

Harry discovered during his career that many people who approved heartily of hanging were still deeply shocked when they discovered he was a hangman. He and his wife were constantly receiving anonymous letters and phone calls – the favourite epithet was "animal." And then there were the tourists.

While he was a hangman Harry always ran a pub, and word soon got around about the landlord's other job. "We had a lot of people in the pub, Americans mostly, who came souvenir hunting and glass buying – looking for anything they could exhibit or sell, even if it's only a visiting card, as long as it's autographed.

"The regular customers protected me against the vultures, as I used to call the sightseers. When the vultures saw me they were often surprised because I suppose I looked so normal. They must have been expecting to see a kind of Frankenstein."

One man who objected to Harry's other job was his father, and as a result father and son became estranged, which was something that hurt Harry deeply. Samuel Allen, a religious man, was appalled when he became aware that his son was working as Pierrepoint's assistant. But public disapprobation never worried him. His wife Marjorie was outwardly calm, and the subject was never mentioned at home.

Harry Allen used to talk about hanging with the same hopeless acceptance with which he described the notoriety it brought to him and his family. He would discuss individual cases with the detachment you might expect from a civil servant putting through a compulsory purchase order. The law was the law; personal judgments or emotions were irrelevant.

"All the officials present feel very, very sorry for the man who's got to go. I mean the prison officers, the chaplain and often the governor. I've seen some very upset cases.

"Everyone is miserable that the man has got into that position but, after all, he's brought it upon himself. And once he's there, there's nothing at all anyone can do about it – except get it over as quickly as possible and forget about it. We've all got a specific job to do that's expected of us, and we just get on and do it."

When the condemned man moves towards the execution cell – known variously as the "dropping shop" or the "topping shed" – he faces the rope for the first time. Beyond it stands the executioner and beyond him a simple crucifix fixed to the cell wall.

"The crucifix reminds the prisoner of what is going to happen to him," said Harry. "Nine out of 10 have their eyes shut as I push the lever and the trap-doors open." And after the execution: "Quite often I'd have to buy an evening paper to find out who I'd hanged."

Asked about the reaction of the condemned, he said: "The night before he's hanged, after his last hope of a reprieve has gone, it's then that he starts examining his spiritual life and forgetting his material life. I think it's only then that he remembers the wrong he has done. He

43

must live his life several times over.

"The men who have to go seem a lot more callous now [this was in 1965, his last year in the job] than in the old days. Quite a few of them are pretty boastful – think they're heroes, I suppose. The other prisoners help this by chanting and banging and kicking up a fuss.

"It's always surprised me a bit, but the condemned man often goes through the whole thing a lot calmer than those doing the job. One man said to me: 'Look at that cloud. I shall be a bloody sight luckier than you tomorrow. I shall be sat on that.' They don't all go as easily as that, but it's the kind of thing that makes you admire their coolness.

"There isn't much time even for a prisoner to say something like that. It's all over so quickly. The man who has to go doesn't feel a thing, and frankly I'd rather have it that way myself than face twelve years inside. I couldn't face that in fact. I think long terms of imprisonment are a much worse form of punishment than hanging."

Harry habitually spoke about himself and the job in this heavy, roundabout language, using a matter-of-fact tone of voce but cloaking his meaning in euphemism. For instance, he hardly ever used the term "condemned man." It was nearly always "the man who has to go."

Despite the impression he gave that capital punishment was painless and sometimes necessary, in the 1960s Harry was briefly an abolitionist. His reason had surprisingly little connection with the reasons cited by abolitionist campaigners. It had nothing to do with the changing climate of opinion; he simply made up his mind that hanging had to a large extent ceased to be a deterrent.

The turning point, he believed, came in the early 1950s. "There was a big change – I noticed it first with a fellow who was hanged in 1956. He was a very arrogant man; and it was becoming the trend with all of them. They were quite proud of what they'd done and willing to do it again.

"When I first started going to prisons they seemed

very sorry for themselves and sorry about what they had done to the other person. Now all that's finished – there aren't any regrets at all."

This kind of callousness, he thought, was particularly noticeable among young murderers. Like many outside observers, he was struck by the case of Victor Terry, who shot a bank clerk just one hour after two youths he knew had been hanged for a brutal and pointless murder. He said of Terry, whose story is told in Chapter 7: "I reckon it was his social acquaintances that drove him to it. I thought he was quite an intelligent lad and not bad deep down."

He noted with increasing astonishment the total lack of remorse among modern murderers. In the old days – he used to talk about them with a rather chilling nostalgia – the condemned man often felt morally obliged to pay for his murder. Gradually this eye-for-an-eye view completely disappeared. Since the murder by Victor Terry of the defenceless bank guard, with its strong element of emulation, his view of the deterrent value of capital punishment was badly shaken. He felt that if you took away any emotional sense of retribution as well the whole thing became pointless.

After the abolition of capital punishment he abandoned his abolitionist stance, probably from sheer desperation at all the increasing violence. It seemed to him then that Britain was set on becoming a lawless country. Many people, especially the elderly, were enraged at declining morality, and the disdain for the law and for other people's lives and property that was prevalent and increasingly seemed to have official sanction. Asked about his view of this when he was 71 years old, Harry declared that the country had changed radically in the 18 years since he retired from the job of public executioner. He said: "I wish it had never been abolished. It seems obvious to me that people must think twice before taking a life if they know they are likely to die themselves. Crimes of violence, armed robbery and horrific killings have escalated."

He admitted to having few emotions about the people

he executed, and could remember most of them only vaguely. "I can shut them out of my mind completely – I could come out of the nick after a hanging and it's all forgotten, and that's the way I like to keep it. When it's finished it's finished. They've paid the price."

CHAPTER 3

FIRST EXECUTION AS THE NEW CHIEF

At all levels of society in the mid-1950s there was a major rethink going on about the purpose of capital punishment, with the result that, from August, 1955, until May, 1957, every convicted murderer in Britain was reprieved. In the nation's assize courts, the black cap had become a meaningless ritual. During this period, Parliament would first attempt to abolish the death penalty and then modify its use.

In November, 1955, Sydney Silverman, MP, introduced a bill to abolish capital punishment. It received its first reading, but as it was a private member's bill, it was given no priority over other parliamentary business and it faded away.

The following year Parliament, at least in the Commons, was divided between retention and abolition. For seven hours the Commons debated a motion, "That this House is of the opinion that, while the death penalty should be retained, the law relating to the crime of murder should be amended." This was a compromise measure designed to retain the death penalty, but the abolitionists would have none of it. Sydney Silverman countered with another motion, "That this House believes that the death penalty for murder no longer accords with the needs or the true interests of a civilised society, and calls on the Government to introduce forthwith legislation for its abolition or suspension for an experimental period." The vote was in favour by 293 to 262.

Looking behind the vote, it is clear that two things influenced it. First, there had been a General Election the previous year, bringing in a number of younger MPs. Second, the execution in July 1955 of Ruth Ellis, the last woman hanged in Britain, was still a newsworthy item creating a focus for abolition.

The balance in the Commons having been tipped, the Death Penalty (Abolition) Bill then proceeded through the parliamentary process. MPs were given a free vote, and the second reading was carried by 286 to 262 – still a narrow majority.

The biggest hurdle had still to be overcome. This was the House of Lords, where the bill was decisively defeated by 238 votes to 95 on July 10th. The death penalty remained suspended, however, and in due time the Government came up with a plan to reduce its scope. This was the Homicide Bill, and because it was a Government bill, as distinct from a private member's bill, it passed through the parliamentary process on party political lines and was approved by the House of Lords.

The bill provided the death penalty for the following murders:

Any murder done in the course of or furtherance of theft; any murder by shooting or causing an explosion; any murder done in the course of or for the purpose of resisting, avoiding or preventing a lawful arrest; of effecting or assisting an escape or rescue from legal custody; any murder of a police officer or a prison officer acting in the execution of his duty or of a person assisting a police officer so acting; in the case of a person who was a prisoner at the time when he did or was party to the murder.

There were also sections on repeated murders, provocation, suicide pacts, diminished responsibility and courts martial.

The bill became law on March 21st, 1957, as the Homicide Act – an acceptable compromise supported by the majority of public opinion.

The protracted capital punishment debate meant that there was no immediate work for Harry Allen. But while death sentences were now being routinely reprieved, one did almost slip through the net. Harry was engaged as assistant in the execution of Thomas Bancroft at Strangeways and the Home Office, apparently oblivious to previous reprieves, confirmed the sentence on December 28th, 1955. Harry duly went to the prison on January 2nd, 1956, where he met Albert Pierrepoint, who was to officiate next morning. That evening, however, it was confirmed that Bancroft would not hang and had received a respite of sentence.

Harry wasn't overly put out by this, but Pierrepoint felt very aggrieved. He asked for his full payment as executioner, and when it wasn't forthcoming he resigned. His letter throwing in the job was dated February 23rd. He had executed more than 450 people.

The Royal Commission on Capital Punishment (1949–1953) had recommended that there should be two principal hangmen, and the Home Office now decided to act on that suggestion, appointing Harry Allen and a Manchester based Scot, Robert Stewart. However, of the two, Harry was regarded as the Number One, and he was to carry out 29 of the last 35 executions in Britain and Ireland before capital punishment in all its forms for murder was finally abolished in 1965. Stewart acted as chief executioner in only six executions after 1957. After the abolition of the death penalty he went to live in South Africa.

For many more months Harry continued to be constantly engaged, and the reprieves continued to be constantly given. This situation would change when a death sentence was pronounced under the new Homicide Act. This happened in mid-summer 1957. Now what, everyone wondered, would a judge and jury make of this latest murder case, where a burglar had to all intents and purposes broken into a sweetshop in the middle of the night to steal, and had murdered the defenceless owner during the course of that crime? Would he be found guilty; more significantly, if he were found guilty would the new Homicide Act be enforced?

The burglar was brought to trial at Cumberland Assizes on May 22nd, 1957, where he pleaded not guilty to the murder. He did not deny killing the sweetshop owner, but claimed that it was manslaughter because he hadn't intended to kill her.

The case, said the prosecutor, Jack di V. Nahum, QC, was one of the first capital murder cases to be brought under the new act – one of five types of murder carrying the death penalty because it was committed in the course of, or furtherance of, theft, and the prosecution needed to prove that there was an intention to steal.

But additionally under the new act, a killing during a robbery was no longer automatically murder as a capital crime, so the prosecution also had to prove that the defendant intended to kill or cause the sweetshop owner grievous bodily harm.

The owner of the sweetshop, Jane Duckett, was so fed up with burglars raiding her premises that she bought a whistle to alert her neighbours in the event of any further trouble. But no one heard anything the night the shop was broken into and Jane was murdered. The reason, it emerged later, was that she had lost her whistle.

The outcome of her loss was to make judicial history in Britain, and to prompt discussions about the criminal justice system that went on for another 30 years.

The burglar who killed 73-year-old Jane just over half a century ago, on Saturday night, April 13th, 1957, got into her Tait Street, Carlisle, shop by breaking the cellar window. He didn't expect to see Jane, who lived in the flat above the shop, because he thought she would be asleep, and he knew she was slightly deaf. While he was still in the cellar he saw a light go on upstairs. He knew then that he had been heard, and that the old lady was coming to investigate. As she came down the stairs he hid in a dark corner, but she spotted him almost at once.

"What are you doing here?" she shrieked.

Although the burglar was 22 years old – more than 50 years younger than Jane – she flew at him, fists raised. The burglar hit her with his clenched fist, and she fell against him. He hit her again and again, losing count of the number of blows he struck.

Jane continued to fight desperately for her life, falling under a rain of blows and kicks, at one stage grabbing the intruder's ankles so that some of the fibre from his socks stayed on her hands. Finally she slumped forward, and as he pushed her away from him she collapsed on the floor.

He left her where she lay, went upstairs to the living-room and ransacked a set of drawers. Although there was £882 hidden in the flat, he found nothing. He was in a hurry because he wasn't sure whether Jane was still alive, and feared she might come after him again. In fact, he had already killed her.

The burglar didn't wait to find that out. He went back to his lodgings, washed the blood from his clothes, cleaned and ironed his tie and went to bed.

Twelve hours later, on Sunday morning, a neighbour, 10-year-old Michael Butcher, noticed an air of abandonment about his favourite sweetshop. The milk was still on the doorstep, the blinds were still down. He told his father, who went to see for himself and, noting that the cellar window was smashed, called the police.

They found Jane dead at the foot of the stairs. At first they thought she might have fallen down the stairs, because although drawers were left open in her living quarters, there was no sign of a struggle. The post-mortem soon disproved that theory – she had been punched and kicked viciously, the pathologist reported. There was also bruising of the neck, consistent with her attacker having gripped her there.

Her close friend told detectives she had invited Jane to stay with her at night following two previous break-ins, which Jane had reported. On those occasions the windows had been smashed, but still the old lady refused to move out. Instead, she bought the whistle, which she subsequently lost.

Although the police appealed to anyone with "even the smallest piece of information" to contact them, they already had a suspect. John Vickers, a 22-year-old labourer, had been taken into custody a few days after the murder, charged with another theft. He was routinely asked about his whereabouts over the weekend of the murder and confessed at once.

"I did it. I don't know what possessed me," he said.

Vickers had been keeping his eye on Jane's shop for some time. He lived in Aglionby Street, just up the road from the sweetshop, and once before he had tried to break in.

His roommate, Robert Watson, told the police that Vickers had often spoken to him about the shop. "The old lady must be making a fortune," he told Watson. When he saw Vickers on Sunday night, the night after the murder, there were scratches on his face. Vickers explained: "I was in Penrith on Saturday night and I got into a fight outside the dance hall."

Police inquiries revealed that there had been no fight at the dance hall that night, so they went to Vickers' home, took away his clothes for examination, and then charged him with murder.

He was readily forthcoming. "I smashed a pane of glass in the cellar window and unfastened it," he said. "The window then crashed down and smashed another pane. I went into the cellar and heard someone coming down.

"I hid, but Miss Duckett saw me and asked me what I was doing. She flew at me and I hit her." While she lay inert on the cellar floor he searched her flat, but he couldn't find any money.

When Vickers was brought into the assize dock it seemed an open and shut case, but it wasn't quite as simple as that.

There seemed to be enough evidence that he was in the sweetshop with intent to steal. The police interviewed a witness who said that a few days before the murder Vickers told him: "Miss Duckett's place would be easy to get into." Vickers had also hinted that there would be more money on the premises at weekends than on weekdays.

As for intent to murder, the prosecutor felt very clear about that. "Surely," he said, "if a man of 22 kicks and punches an old lady of 73 he intends to cause her grievous bodily harm. If you are satisfied Vickers did this, then he murdered her." The prosecutor suggested there was evidence of intention to steal because a drawer was pulled out in the old lady's living-room, and the contents scattered on the floor. Two other drawers were open.

Hours before the murder Vickers did go to a Saturday night dance in Penrith, but a procession of witnesses told the court there was no fight there, rejecting Vickers' claim that he was scratched on the face during an affray. An RAF man who gave him a lift back to Carlisle testified that his passenger's face was unmarked. He dropped Vickers off near the sweetshop at 1 a.m.

A Home Office forensic scientist told the court that the wool of Vickers' socks was identical to a green fibre found in Jane Duckett's hand.

Giving evidence on his own behalf, Vickers denied kicking Jane Duckett. He did not realise she was likely to die or might be dead, and he did not become concerned until the middle of Sunday morning, when he noticed that the blinds of her shop were still closed. That afternoon he learned that "Ma" Duckett had been killed. He agreed he lied in his first statement to the police.

"I don't know why I hit her," he told the jury. "It was just panic and I was afraid she might recognise me."

Mr. Nahum put to him: "If you were prosecuted for breaking and entering the premises, you wanted to make certain that she would never be able to give evidence against you?"

Vickers replied: "No, sir."

"But that is what has happened, isn't it?"

"Yes, sir."

"Why did you hit her so often? What were you trying to do?"

"I don't know."

"You knew perfectly well she was dead before you risked going upstairs and searching the apartment?"

"I didn't know she was dead."

"When you were raining blows on her, didn't you appreciate that as she was a woman of 73 you were bound to do her serious injury?"

"No, sir."

"She could not have got that fibre of wool unless she was lying on the floor and put her hands up to her face as you kicked her?"

"She might, but I did not kick her."

Was there anything he did that could have caused the bruising on Jane's neck, he was asked? But again, it was, "I don't know."

Summing-up, Mr. Justice Hinchcliffe said that in considering whether the case was one of capital murder or manslaughter, the jury should take the view of "a reasonable man." What would such a man think of an attack by a fit and strong young man on a frail old lady?

The jury returned after a brief retirement to find Vickers guilty of capital murder. The new act had changed the form of the death sentence. There was now no ritualistic performance telling the prisoner he would be "hanged by the neck until you are dead," but instead he would "suffer death in the manner authorised by law."

Vickers decided to appeal. His claim was based on the contention that the judge misdirected the jury in his remarks about the Homicide Act. The defence claimed that a murder committed with the intention of causing grievous bodily harm, entailed "constructive malice," which had been abolished by the act.

Pleading the case for the prosecution in the Appeal Court, Sir Reginald Manningham-Buller, the Attorney-General, who had been instrumental in drafting the act, contended that any death resulting from "serious harm" had always been "murder and nothing else," and this was still the case.

That there was still serious confusion even among judges was revealed when the Appeal Court judges were unable to agree. They decided they would have another meeting, when all five judges would discuss the appeal. What sort of law was this, people wondered, when even those who had to implement it couldn't understand it? Enter, then, the Lord Chief Justice, to announce that in his view the judge's summing-up had been impeccable and Vickers' appeal was dismissed.

This was how it worked out. In the opinion of the Lord Chief Justice, Vickers had to die because "if a person does an act which amounts to the infliction of grievous bodily ham, he cannot say he intended only to cause a certain or less degree of harm...and he must take the consequences.

"If he intended to inflict grievous bodily harm and his victim died, that has always been held in English law sufficient to imply malice aforethought, which is the necessary constituent of murder."

In other words, nothing had really changed. If you beat someone up with the intention of causing them serious harm and they die, then that's murder, and always was.

John Vickers was among the many people in Britain who were convinced he wouldn't hang. Many Tory MPs – the Conservatives were in office – had voted to retain hanging in the belief that it would be imposed only in exceptional circumstances and that it would fall into abeyance.

But Home Secretary R. A. Butler wouldn't be swayed by popular opinion, not even in his own party, and to the astonishment of many people Vickers became the first person to be executed under the new Homicide Act when Harry Allen hanged him on July 23rd, 1957, at Durham Prison.

The condemned man's last visitor was his distraught mother. The night before the execution six MPs participated in a silent prayer meeting in London that went on through the night.

For Harry it was a special day in his career. Because of the passage of the act through Parliament, his previous two executions had been cancelled. The first person convicted of capital murder under the act was Ronald Dunbar, at Newcastle. The Home Office wrote to Harry on May 16th, 1957, giving an execution date of June 6th. Dunbar subsequently appealed and the execution never went ahead.

He was next engaged to execute Franklin McPherson

on July 16th but this execution too was never carried out.

With that sort of history since the act was passed, there did seem every reason to expect that Vickers would be reprieved too. When that didn't happen, the execution of the man whose career had been built on thieving – Vickers' first conviction for theft was when he was 11 – became Harry's first-ever job as chief executioner. He wrote in his diary: "First execution for two years, a very good job, best ever done at the above," referring to Durham Prison.

Six thousand people gathered outside the prison by 9 a.m. The ticking clock was their only indication of when it was all over – under the new act no execution notice was posted on the prison gates. As Harry left he was recognised, and a large lady stepped out of the crowd and stabbed him with her umbrella, pushing a large hole through his bowler hat. She was Mrs. Violet van der Elste, Britain's most vociferous campaigner against capital punishment. This was not her day of triumph – but that day was not so far distant.

The second and last execution of 1957 took place at Birmingham Prison on December 4th. The condemned man was Dennis Howard, who shot dead David Keasey during a shop robbery. Harry was contacted by the Under Sheriff of Worcestershire to confirm the date in a letter of November 19th. Harry recorded the execution in his diary as "Very good." He was assisted by Royston Rickard, of Maidstone, and also present were Harry Robinson of Stafford and Thomas Cunliffe of Wigan. They were both trained at Pentonville Prison in June, 1956, but this was the first time they had witnessed an execution prior to their names being added to the Home Office list.

The House of Lords resurrected the case of John Vickers in 1981. They decided to inquire whether there had been a miscarriage of justice and whether he had been rightly convicted. They came to the conclusion that their predecessors had made all the right decisions.

CHAPTER 4

EXECUTION OF A SCOTTISH SERIAL KILLER

Harry's second wife Doris was to observe that she could never get her husband to go abroad on holiday – not, at least, until he had given up hanging. But in 1957 the Home Office appeared to have no difficulty in dispatching their new chief executioner to a distant land.

This was Cyprus, which was having a turbulent time in the 1950s. Both the communities on the island, Turkish and Greek, were under British administration. Most of the Greek community favoured union with Greece, but because of strategic matters and diplomatic relations with Turkey the British could not allow that to happen.

Union with Greece was called Enosis, and demand for it led to a paramilitary insurgency by a Greek Cypriot group called EOKA. The political leader of Enosis was Archbishop Makarios, while EOKA was under the command of a former Greek army colonel, George Grivas.

Britain reacted with military action to counter civil disorder and paramilitary attacks – the mayhem was exacerbated by open hostility between the Greek and Turkish communities. When political talks failed, Archbishop Makarios was exiled to the Seychelles, in March, 1956. The paramilitary attacks then escalated, and a state of emergency, which allowed the use of the death penalty for crimes other than murder, was declared.

So it was that in a letter dated December 31st, 1957, the Colonial Office formally requested Harry's services:

Sir,
Your name has been given to this department by the Prison Commission, and I am directed by Mr. Secretary Lennox-

Boyd to inquire whether you would be prepared to carry out any hangings which might be necessary in Cyprus. The average number of executions, excluding those connected with the present emergency, is less than two per annum.

I am to explain that the apparatus used in Cyprus is basically the same as that in use in the United Kingdom, although it is by no means new and does not incorporate such improvements as may have been introduced in the United Kingdom in recent years. It could however probably be remedied without great difficulty.

If you are willing to undertake such assignments, the Cyprus Government would pay your fares, subsistence allowance while in Cyprus, and fees in accordance with those laid down for executions in the United Kingdom. Experienced expatriate assistance is already available in Cyprus but if it was considered necessary, the Cyprus Government will also engage an assistant from the United Kingdom.

A stamped address envelope was enclosed for a reply, which undoubtedly was in the affirmative because in September, 1958, Harry flew to Cyprus to hang terrorist Nicos Sampson, a Greek gunman who publicly boasted how he shot down British soldiers.

Harry, with his assistant Harry Smith, called to collect Sampson from the death cell at Central Prison, Nicosia, on September 10th. The hangman's "box of tricks" – a wooden crate containing the regulation rope and leather straps – had already been flown from England.

A witness said: "The hangman and his assistant arrived at the condemned cell on the stroke of midnight. All they needed was confirmation from the prison governor to go ahead. They stood there for what must have seemed a very long 15 minutes.

"Then the governor arrived with a message from the Governor of Cyprus, Sir John Harding, to say it was all off. That was a close thing." Later, after the British relinquished the reins of government, Nicos Sampson became President of Cyprus. And Harry Allen, who came within seconds of hanging him, went back to Lancashire.

•

Peter Manuel was already on trial for eight murders in Scotland when a detective from England travelled to Glasgow to confer with his Scottish colleagues.

"Manuel is wanted in England for another murder," he explained. "So in the unlikely event that he's acquitted, I'm here to re-arrest him."

The ninth murder was the cold-blooded killing of a Newcastle taxi-driver, for it was to Newcastle that Manuel went the previous year, in December, 1957, equipped with a gun and a well-honed knife, on his release from Barlinnie Prison in Scotland. Alighting from the train at Newcastle station, he hailed a cab. Sidney Dunn, well wrapped up in scarf and overcoat, drew up at the wheel of his taxi to pick up the fare.

"Take me to Edmundbyers," Manuel told the cabbie. At least that is what Dunn thought he said, but the police later came to think that in his thick Glasgow accent Manuel had given Edinburgh as his destination, Dunn mishearing him. The taxi accordingly began making its way south-west out of Newcastle, heading for the moorland village of Edmundbyers.

After a while, detectives later speculated, Manuel realised he was going in the wrong direction. As the taxi approached Edmundbyers he decided he had gone far enough. Choosing a suitably isolated spot along the road, he told the driver to stop. He stepped out of the cab, turned, and calmly shot the driver in the head. Sidney Dunn slumped forward, his face masked with blood.

But Manuel hadn't finished. Sticking his gun in his pocket he took out his knife and, pulling the driver's scarf aside, slit his throat. He wiped the knife on the grass verge and then walked off across the moor, disappearing into the mist.

He was known to have spent three weeks in England at that time. He also became the prime suspect in two other murders south of the Scottish border.

Sidney Dunn's killing was to remain on the file

because a further trial for Peter Manuel was rendered unnecessary by the outcome of his court appearance in Scotland.

From the moment the Scottish trial of Peter Manuel began it was scheduled to be big – very big indeed, perhaps the crime case of the century. *True Detective* magazine's correspondent and criminologist Nigel Morland, who attended the court, went to Manuel's house, talked to thieves and gangsters, and interviewed policemen to get himself a full picture of what happened and what drove this callous killer. This account of Manuel's life is based on Morland's story.

Peter Thomas Anthony Manuel was born in New York City on March 15th, 1926. His father Samuel Manuel had emigrated there with his wife when jobs were hard to get in Scotland. Five years later in 1932 the Manuel family returned to Motherwell in Lanarkshire. Peter was even then a brash, tough little boy. He was a big handful at school, and he didn't in the least resemble his mild-mannered older brother or his sister. When in 1937 the family moved south to Coventry he really began to break loose.

His name became a by-word for trouble at St. Elizabeth's Roman Catholic School. He was caught cheating, told lies and, when the headmistress found an "unspeakably filthy" drawing on her desk, instead of being remorseful for what he had done Manuel became truculent.

Not long after that he broke into the church adjoining St. Elizabeth's and rifled the offertory boxes.

In the same year he was charged with housebreaking and theft from a local greyhound stadium, and by the time he was 15 no fewer than 19 charges had been laid against him. The offences had continued not for want of punishment – he escaped eight times from approved schools. On his 16th birthday he committed robbery, fraud and indecent assault.

He was still in his teens when he returned to Motherwell. He was now an old lag and an enigma.

Dark, with good looks and extremely wide shoulders,

he could turn on the charm when he felt like it. He was a passionate reader, with a depth of knowledge about notorious American gangsters. His friends claimed that he could "talk the leg off a mule," and he had a native wit and a fresh turn of phrase coupled with an ingenious mind. Yet he refused to be restrained by the ordinary civilised boundaries of life.

Manuel saw himself as a sort of criminal mastermind – a larger than life portrayal of the criminals he read so much about. But there was a seamy side to his criminality. He attacked women and young girls in the dark streets near his home. Once he attacked a nurse. She gave the police an excellent description of Peter Manuel, but was unable to pick him out in an identification parade.

The attacks continued unabated, and although Manuel apparently kept his head down working as a labourer, the buzz was that he was responsible for a lot of thieving, and a few rapes as well.

When the police finally had enough evidence to arrest him, he faced 18 charges of theft. While he was on bail he attacked and raped a married woman while she was on her way home along a dark road.

Questioned, he denied all knowledge of the attack, and claimed he wasn't in the area at the time. But the facts were damning. Unusual soil at the point of the attack matched dirt found on his shoes, and red and green fibres on his clothing matched threads on the red and green scarf the victim was wearing.

He was charged with housebreaking, theft and rape. Aged only 19, he was sentenced to nine years, disappearing into the living hell of Peterhead Prison.

Prisoners do not like sex offenders. Old lags can be as peculiar about their associates as any social climber, and in those days no "respectable" crook would be seen dead in the company of a rapist. Manuel was lucky. Because of his youth, the inmates of Peterhead decided to let him off. He was left alone – until, that is, he went for a Glasgow razor king who insulted him.

He came off worse, but at least earned the friendship

of a Lanarkshire safe-blowing mob. Because Lanarkshire men were in those days the aristocracy of jails, Manuel had an easier time after that.

For nearly six years he behaved reasonably well, until a box of dinner knives went missing. The trusties whose job it was to issue the knives at meal times were all under suspicion until a squeak reached the authorities. Manuel was accused, and was punished with a few days on bread and water.

When he came out of the punishment block he was undoubtedly seeing himself as a sort of prison hero. Instead of coasting along with authority and keeping out of trouble, he went for a warder at the first opportunity, tore his cell to pieces, and climbed out on to a balcony where he began smashing porridge bowls.

It took a squad of strong-arm men to subdue him. This time they sent him to the snake pit, the punishment cell where bed was a wooden board, a small tree stump served as the only chair, and the prisoner was in total isolation.

One visitor was allowed – a Catholic priest who tried to comfort him. Manuel rejected his ministrations, insisting that he was an atheist committed to communism. He was probably showing off, but he did not fail to make it convincing.

He had developed a vast contempt for policemen and prison warders. Doctors sent to examine him did not realise that he had been in trouble with the police since childhood. He was steeped in American gangster lore; he also realised that he had homosexual tendencies and could do nothing about it.

His associates had varying views about his sexual balance. Some said he was impotent, others that he was bisexual, while another, claiming to know him well, said he obtained satisfaction only through groping.

What he decided to be at any given time depended on his prevailing mental image. Whatever his fantasy, so he was. If he saw himself as a rapist, a burglar, a murderer, or a gunman, that was what he became. But for the moment he was out of prison on release, and to earn a living he became a railway shunter.

His friends called him "the biggest liar in Lanarkshire," and although he was well aware of this reputation it never stopped him telling endless fairy tales, even to the extent of claiming to be the mastermind behind most of the big criminal jobs at the time. This was sometimes believable, because Manuel's speech had none of the customary vulgarity of the crook; he was scrupulously clean in his appearance, fastidious about his clothes, and had excellent manners.

His memory was almost photographic and his mind was extraordinarily well stocked – he could simulate a good educational background. He could play the piano, drew well, and knew a fair amount about astronomy. While he was a mean and vicious criminal, at times he could be kind and generous.

When he fell genuinely in love for the first time, late in 1953, the girl was a strict Roman Catholic from an equally strict family. When Manuel announced to her parents that he too was a Catholic – he was certainly born into Catholicism – he was given the freedom of the girl's home, where his courtesy was highly regarded.

The affair was serious and marriage discussions were frequent, but although they were always together Manuel never took the girl into his inner circle of friends. No doubt he didn't want her to know too much about his background.

His mean streak showed itself when the girl chose an expensive engagement ring, which, between the jeweller's shop and her hand, became a cheap imitation. Perhaps this isn't an unheard-of action for an impoverished young man in love, but what stamps it as ugly was that Manuel openly boasted about this duplicity to his friends.

The duplicity came to an abrupt end when, one day in July, 1955, his fiancée received a letter telling her all about Manuel's prison record. She broke off the engagement. How much this upset Manuel is a matter for conjecture, but it certainly happened that only days later he attacked a young woman. She had been to a dance hall, expecting to meet friends there. But they failed to arrive, so she set off for home along a lonely road on her own.

Suddenly, without any warning, hands closed around her face and she was dragged to a field close to a tiny shop on the nearby main road. Her attacker spoke gruffly and warned her not to struggle, although she managed one loud call for help.

The girl was clear-minded enough to try to remember the man's voice for future identification. He forced her on to the grass and fondled her in a way that she later described as nauseating.

John Buchanan, owner of a nearby shop, heard her call for help. He went out searching with a torch, and at the sound of his approaching footsteps Manuel smashed his fist into the girl's face, warning her to stay silent. The torch beam passed within a few feet of where she was being held down on the grass.

She was beaten again as she was dragged across the field. Manuel sat down beside her, lit a cigarette, and by way of explanation told her, "My girl has let me down." He then bizarrely offered to take her to the police station. He escorted her back to the road, and would have walked her home if she hadn't resolutely declined.

She realised from the light of his match when he lit the cigarette that he was a passenger on the bus she took to work. She complained to the police and Manuel was arrested. But at his trial he defended himself with such adroitness that he confused the arresting officers about the clothes he was wearing at the time of the attack. And when the judge warned him about the dangers of introducing new evidence, he coolly went ahead and did so.

So deftly did he tie up the case, employing the gestures of what John Buchanan, the shopkeeper, called "a third-rate actor," that the jury were hopelessly confused, to such an extent that their verdict was "not proven."

The real sufferer was his victim, who became the target for much malicious gossip. While she waited for her bus on the morning after the trial, a member of the Manuel family came up and spat in her face.

The ugliest phase of the Manuel story began towards the end of 1955. He was working near East Kilbride golf course as an assistant pipe layer for the gas board when in a nearby copse of fir trees, police discovered the body of Anne Kneilands. She had been so severely battered to death that blood was spattered to a height of 20 feet on one of the fir trees. She had not been raped and not even been interfered with – but it was instantly noted that Peter Manuel was working within close proximity to the crime scene, and that he had arrived at work the morning after the murder with scratches on his face.

He was questioned for four hours, but steadfastly denied all knowledge of the murder. The scratches, he explained, resulted from a fight in Glasgow. He was so confident that he would not be charged that he agreed to allow a local newspaper to publish his photograph as one of the people who had been questioned. No one came forward to say they had seen him in East Kilbride at the time of the murder. The bluff worked – there was insufficient evidence to charge him.

Manuel next broke into a colliery canteen with another man, who was caught when they were disturbed. Manuel got away, but left a fragment of his jacket on a barbed wire fence.

He had taken to carrying a gun, and the wiser heads among the criminal fraternity avoided him, aware of what might happen to a man – and his associates – when a weapon was part of the equipment for a burglary.

The law caught up with him in September, 1956, when the fragment of coat on the barbed wire was analysed and traced to him as the other burglar at the colliery canteen. He was charged with burglary and indicted for trial.

But only a few days later he was drinking with friends when he suddenly announced that he had to leave "on a job." The nature of the "job" wasn't specified, but that same day death came to a local family, when Mrs. Marion Watt, her sister Margaret and her 16-year-old daughter Vivienne were shot dead by a burglar in their bungalow in Fennsbank Avenue, Uddingston. The slaughter was wanton and pitiless, the work of a cool and steady psychopath.

A police car arrived at Manuel's house the following night and while he was still in his pyjamas officers interrogated him. Finally he turned on them and snapped, "Either charge me, or stop persecuting me!"

They didn't charge him. Ten days later they arrested William Watt for the murder of his family. Watt claimed he was 80 miles away at the time of the slaughter in his bungalow, but he was nevertheless brought before Glasgow Sheriff Court, while police held back an angry mob demonstrating outside.

On October 2nd Manuel stood in the dock at Hamilton Sheriff Court and was sentenced to 18 months for the colliery burglary. At the same time and in the same building police officers were preparing appeals for public help in a fresh attempt to find the murderer of Anne Kneilands.

Manuel was sent to Barlinnie Prison, where as fate would have it, William Watt was being held on remand, awaiting his trial for a triple-murder. Manuel promptly wrote to Watt's solicitor and told him that he knew Watt was innocent. When he repeated this statement at Watt's trial, the Crown, suitably impressed, withdrew all the charges against William Watt.

Manuel claimed that a convict in Peterhead Prison named Charles Tallis, and two other men, had planned to break into a bungalow in Fennsbank Avenue, where a wealthy family lived. They planned to shoot all the occupants save one, who was to be forced into revealing the hiding place of a lot of money.

Unfortunately, he explained, Tallis and his friends got their bungalows mixed up, and the wrong people died.

William Watt got his freedom, but he wasn't taken in by Manuel's story. He was pretty sure that Charles Tallis was Peter Manuel, particularly when Manuel was able to describe to him the details of the Watt home.

The story demonstrates how Manuel continually

flirted with risks. Contemptuous of the police, and certain that he would never be caught, he broke into a house in Mount Vernon simply to show off. He took nothing, but cooked himself a meal before he left.

On New Year's Eve he was with his family playing the dutiful son and the affectionate brother, and phoning his sister at her workplace to sing her a popular song in Italian. That night he slept on a downstairs divan, and was in the process of just waking up when his mother came down in the morning. She had no way of knowing that during that same night a whole family had been shot dead in a nearby bungalow. They were the Smarts – the father, mother, and their 12-year-old son.

Between the night of the murders, and January 6th, when they first came to light, a neighbour distinctly remembered the curtains having moved several times in the bungalow. This could only have indicated that Manuel had returned more than once to gloat over the scene of slaughter.

His next victim was 17-year-old Isabelle Cooke, who vanished after going to a hockey club dance.

Clues began to surface and, significantly, a pointer came from William Watt, who showed detectives a bullet he found in a mattress in his bungalow. It turned out to be a .38-calibre, and had been fired from the Webley revolver used in the Watt family murders.

Next, a man was traced who had sold Peter Manuel a Beretta, the type of gun used in the Smart family murders. Detectives also learned that Manuel had suddenly come into possession of £30, the exact sum stolen from the Smarts' bungalow.

On January 14th, 1958, the police raided Manuel's home and took away articles stolen from the house in Mount Vernon. When Manuel's father claimed that the articles belonged to him he was whisked away and locked up, while his son was put on an identification parade at Hamilton police station. After that he was charged with the murder of the Smart family.

Manuel, it seems, began to realise that the fact that both he and his father were in jail would have an adverse impact on his mother. He asked to see his parents and in the presence of detectives told them: "I have never been able to talk to you. I have had to fight this thing alone. There is no future for me. I have done some terrible things."

What all the terrible things were would emerge later, but first he took officers to a desolate field near North Mount Vernon, a field with a border of gaunt trees between it and a narrow dirt road. There, under recently ploughed land, was the body of Isabelle Cooke, lying where Manuel had murdered her.

Back at police headquarters he wrote a long, detailed confession filled with details that only a guilty man would have known: "I hereby confess that on January 1st, 1956, I was the person responsible for killing Anne Kneilands. On September 17th, 1956, I was responsible for killing Mrs. Marion Watt and her sister Mrs. George Brown, also her daughter, Vivienne. On December 28th, 1957, I was responsible for killing Isabelle Cooke.

"On January 1st, 1958, I was responsible for killing Mr. Peter Smart, his wife Doris and their son.

"On January 1st, 1956, I was in East Kilbride at 7 p.m. About 7.30 I was walking towards the cross when I met a girl. She spoke to me and addressed me as Tommy, and she said she thought she knew me. We got talking, and she told me she had to meet someone, but she did not think they would turn up.

"After a while I asked her if she would like some tea or coffee, and we went into a café. When we came out she said she was going home and I offered to take her home. She said she lived miles away and I would probably get lost if I saw her home. But I insisted, and she said: 'All right.' We walked along a road up to Maxwelltown Road. There we went along a curved road, which I can't remember the name of.

"About half way along the road I pulled her into a field, and she struggled and ran away. I chased her across the field and over a ditch. When I caught up with her I dragged her into a wood and in the wood she started screaming, and I hit her over the head with a piece of iron I picked up."

The confession went on to describe the events of the night of September 16th–17th, 1956.

"When I arrived home I met a man I knew and he took me in a car to High Burnside. He had got another man and woman in the car. They broke into No. 18 Fennsbank Avenue.

"We were there for some time and someone went to bed. I did not know much about the house. The car was left in a lane. After a while I went scouting about looking at the other houses. I found a house that looked empty, and then went back to see the others at No. 18.

"Someone had got the car around. I told them to drive me to the other house. I got out, but the others did not like the look of it and went back. I broke into the house by breaking a glass panel on the front door. I then went in and opened a bedroom door. There were two people in the bed. I went into the other room and there was a girl there. She woke up and sat up. I hit her on the chin and knocked her out.

"I tied her hands and went back to the other room. I shot the two people there, and then heard someone making a noise in the other room. The girl had got loose. We struggled, and I threw her on the bed and shot her.

"I then went back to No. 18 Fennsbank Avenue and found them all asleep. I took the car after waking them, and they dropped me at home about 5 a.m. I did not steal anything from No. 5.

"That same day I went into Glasgow and flung the gun into the Clyde at the Suspension Bridge. I'd got it in a public house called the Merkit Bar at Glasgow Cross."

Manuel then recalled the murder of Isabelle Cooke.

"On December 28th, 1957, I went to Mount Vernon about 7 p.m., going by bus from Birkenshaw to Mount Vernon. I walked up the road leading to the railway bridge that runs from Bothwell to Shettleston. Just over the bridge I met a girl walking. I grabbed her and dragged her into a field on the same side as Ryelands

Riding School. I took her along with me, following a line going in the Bothwell direction.

"I then made her go with me along towards the dog track. When we got near the dog track she started to scream. I tore off her clothes, tied something around her neck, and choked her.

"I then carried her up the line into a field and dug a hole with a shovel. While I was doing this a man passed along the line on a bike so I carried her again over the path opposite the brickworks into another field.

"I dug a hole in the part of the field that was ploughed and put her in it. I covered her up and went back the way I had come. I went back to the road and got her shoes, which had come off at the outset. I took these and her clothes and scattered them about. The clothes I flung in the River Calder at Broomhouse, the shoes I hid on the railway bank at the dog track.

"On the morning of January 1st, I left my home about 5.30 a.m. I went down the path to the foot of the brae crossing the road into Sheepburn Road and broke into the bungalow.

"I went through the house and took a quantity of banknotes from a wallet I found in a jacket in the front bedroom. There was about £20 to £25 in the wallet. I then shot the man in the bed and next the woman. I then went into the next room and shot the boy."

Both the Webley and the Beretta were recovered from the Clyde by a diver.

Interest in Manuel's subsequent trial was so intense that special admission cards were printed in order to allocate the limited accommodation. Queues for admission to the public section of Glasgow's North Court began to form more than 14 hours before the trial began on May 12th, 1959. People brought sandwiches, coffee and folding chairs in preparation for camping out all night on the pavement.

Newly released inmates of Barlinnie Prison supplied a stream of information about the accused to newspapermen, in exchange for cash, of course. One man who was on bail and was expecting to be jailed for housebreaking offered reporters a news service to be provided at visiting time once he was behind bars. In return he wanted his customers to pay a weekly wage to his family.

Manuel appeared in the dock dressed impeccably in a new black blazer, blue trousers, grey shirt and tie. He pleaded not guilty to all the charges against him.

Repudiating his confession, he claimed he was at home with visitors when the Smarts were murdered, and that William Watt was responsible for the murder of his own family.

William Watt, who went into the witness-box on crutches following a car accident, described meeting with Manuel. "I said that if I thought he had anything to do with the tragedy at Burnside [i.e., at the Watt family home] I would not only lay hands on him, I would tear him into little pieces. Manuel sat bolt upright and replied, 'People don't do that to Peter Manuel.'"

The pathologist who examined all eight murder victims produced part of Anne Kneilands' skull and demonstrated how a piece of iron bar fitted one of the fractures. She had received 12 separate injuries.

He said that Isabelle Cooke was strangled by ligatures tied round her mouth and neck, while the Smarts had died instantly, shot in the head as they slept. The Watt family suffered a variety of wounds. Mrs. Watt was shot once in the head; her sister was shot twice, and her daughter was punched in the face as well as shot.

Detective Inspector Robert McNeil told how, after his arrest, Manuel had asked to see his parents. "He said, 'Bring my father and mother here and I'll see them in your presence and after that make a clean breast of it to them. Then I'll clear up everything for you and take you to where the girl Cooke is buried.'"

Describing how Manuel told his parents he had committed eight murders, the inspector said: "He was subdued. I would say he was in a mood of what I might call repentance. He was sorry not only for his position but for the trouble he was giving his family."

When they arrived at the field where Isabelle Cooke

was buried, Manuel stopped at one point and pointing to the ground said: "She is in there. I think I am standing on her."

On the 10th day of the trial Manuel sprang a surprise by dismissing his defence counsel and announcing that he intended to conduct his own defence from the dock. He had little to lose. His counsel had failed in their efforts to have his confession declared inadmissible as evidence, and by now the outcome of the trial was almost a foregone conclusion. What he gained by representing himself was one last memorable ego-trip.

He would now appear, at least to some extent, to be a man in charge of his destiny, taking on the full majesty of the law single-handed. It was his last chance to shine, and he made the most of it. His questions to witnesses were fired swiftly and fluently, and his formidable memory enabled him to cross-examine without referring to documents. He displayed all the calmness and assurance of a courtroom veteran, which, in a way, he was.

His first barrage of questions to police witnesses failed in their attempt, however, to get detectives to concede that they threatened or otherwise intimidated him in order to get a confession. "At no time at all when I was with you did I make any threats to you or put any suggestion in your mind," said the detective inspector who wrote down the confession.

Manuel then told the court he was dissatisfied with his counsel's cross-examination of William Watt. He wanted to give the man he had accused of murdering his own family another grilling, and Watt appeared this time in a wheelchair. Manuel's questions were, in effect, accusations, which Watt dismissed as atrocious lies.

Other questions were disallowed by the judge – as when Manuel asked a retired police superintendent: "Did you feel confident when you arrested Watt that you had arrested the man who shot his wife?" Instructing the detective not to answer, the judge, Lord Cameron, told Manuel: "What this witness may believe or think about any of the charges on which you stand indicted is entirely irrelevant."

Manuel nodded. "Yes, your honour," he said. "I stand corrected." Simply by posing the question, however, he had indicated that when Watt was arrested the police must have believed him to be the killer.

Calling his parents as witnesses, Manuel got his mother to agree that at the police station after his arrest she heard him say, "I don't know why I do these things." Samuel Manuel told the court that he believed the police were prompting his son.

Manuel then left the dock and went into the witness-box to testify on his own behalf. He said he had challenged detectives to hold an identification parade when he was interrogated about Anne Kneilands' murder. He knew nothing of the Watt family murders until he saw a report in a newspaper, and he claimed that Watt had confessed to him that he shot his wife.

He was at a Glasgow cinema the night Isabelle Cooke was murdered, he said, and it was the police who had taken him to the burial site – he was not their guide.

And the Smarts? He sold Mr. Smart a gun, and Mr. Smart gave him a key to his bungalow, inviting him to call. When he took up the invitation he found the family had been shot dead, and he took the gun from Mr. Smart's hand because it was the weapon he had sold to him. A few days later he phoned the police anonymously to tell them what they would find at the Smarts' home.

He wrote his confession only to save his family from police persecution. The whole prosecution case was a conspiracy against him.

After the prosecutor made his final address to the jury, Manuel responded with a speech that demonstrated that whatever else he might be, he was no fool. The range of his vocabulary was amazing, given his background. Although what he had to say was no more than a summary of his earlier arguments, his address was an adroit performance.

Even the judge had to admit to that. Summing up, Lord Cameron said the defendant had presented his own defence "with a skill that is quite remarkable."

The judge went on to direct the jury to acquit Manuel of the murder of Anne Kneilands, due to insufficient corroborative evidence.

Two and a half hours after their retirement, on May 29th, 1958, the jury returned to find Manuel guilty of the other seven murders, and the death sentence was pronounced. Having appeared totally at ease throughout his trial, blithely bounding up the stairs from the cells to the dock, he now turned on his heel and swiftly descended to the cells. His moment of glory was over.

He had fought for his life and lost, and he was not the sort of man who basked in a loser's limelight.

When his appeal failed, Harry Allen was waiting for him at Barlinnie Prison on July 11th, 1958. Manuel had his last breakfast and a glass of whisky before briskly striding the 12 steps from the condemned cell to the execution chamber.

Harry didn't like Manuel. "He was a hard case, a cocky so-and-so when I saw him the day before his execution," he later recalled. "He strutted round the exercise yard like a peacock. But he was a different man when I walked into his cell next morning.

"He trembled and said: 'Have I really got to go?' I tied his hands together and replied: 'Yes, you certainly have.' As I marched him to the scaffold he said, 'In that case, let's get on with it.' He wanted to pretend he was still in charge of the situation. How little he knew!"

It has been suggested that Harry's son Brian assisted him at Manuel's execution, but Brian wasn't on the official list of executioners and the suggestion is an understandable error. What was happening that morning of July 11th was that Marjorie Allen had decided to leave her husband, taking Brian and his younger sister with her. Brian tried to contact his father in Barlinnie Prison to tell him that there was turmoil on the domestic front, but he was initially dismissed as a crank. After getting police friends to confirm his identity he finally got through to his father with the news. By then Harry had hanged Manuel.

It is probable that some official records show Brian

Allen's name as someone trying to contact Harry Allen, leading to Brian being set down as an "assistant."

What, then, was going on behind the scenes at the Junction Hotel? Harry said: "I've always had my fair share of poison pen letters and cranky phone calls. I never read beyond the first few lines and threw the letters on the fire. It didn't bother me because I've always had a clear conscience about my duties. But I think the strain was too much for Marjorie.

"We had an unspoken rule that we never discussed my business as a hangman. I knew she didn't like it. I'd simply tell her I was going away for a few days. She knew what that meant.

"When I set off for Glasgow to hang Peter Manuel, as usual she didn't say a word. But on my return I found she had packed her bags and left, taking Brian and Christine with her.

"She has never given me a word of explanation why she left me. But I believe it was the pressure from the anti-hanging campaigners."

CHAPTER 5

A BRACE OF COP KILLERS

As Harry Allen settled into his bed in the executioner's quarters in Pentonville Prison in the evening of May 7th, 1959, an interminable racket began to fill the prison from end to end.

Allen couldn't sleep. But nor could the man he had come to hang in the morning. This was Ronald Henry Marwood, who had killed a policeman in an affray.

The noise caused by other prisoners cat-calling and banging on their cell walls was a traditional prisoners' demonstration the night before an execution. Marwood may have been pleased with their rather pointless support but he was desperately tired. He asked a warder to request the prisoners to stop the racket. It was the last night of his life, he said, and he wanted some sleep.

After that the noise subsided and the condemned man and his hangman slept the rest of the night peacefully.

Then as now, back in the 1950s London had no shortage of feuding gangs spoiling for a fight. Any trivial slight, whether real or imagined, was enough to trigger violence, and after one gang leader flicked a spill of paper at another one night at a Highbury dance hall in December, 1958, the two gangs, having arranged to settle the matter on the night of the 14th, armed themselves with hatchets, coshes, knives and knuckledusters.

For the gang members, the date had no special significance. But for Ronald Marwood, a 6 ft 2 in, 25-year-old foreman scaffolder living in Pentonville only 400 yards from the prison where he was to hang, it was a red-letter day: the first anniversary of his wedding. His wife Rosalie, however, was feeling unwell that night, so instead of going out with him to celebrate she decided to spend the evening at home while he went out to have a few drinks with his friend Mike Bloom, the best man at the couple's wedding.

After calling at two pubs, where Marwood downed 20 half-pints of brown ale, the two men moved on to Seven Sisters Road in Holloway, where their arrival coincided with the two gangs' confrontation outside Gray's Dance Academy. Neither of the two men were gang members, but somehow they got caught up in the battle that ensued, Marwood receiving cuts on two fingers from a flailing hatchet.

Moments later, Police Constable Raymond Henry Summers, 23, and an impressive 6 ft 4 in, arrived on the scene to break up the fight. When Marwood saw him leading Mike Bloom away, he stepped forward to intervene.

"Clear off!" Summers told him. Next moment the officer was staggering round on the pavement, before collapsing. He had been fatally stabbed in the back.

The warring gangs promptly fled. Marwood ran down a side street and climbed over a garden wall, where he hid, waiting for the commotion to subside. When he began to move on with another fugitive who had joined him, they were stopped by two policemen and taken in for questioning.

"Where have you been?" they were asked.

Both replied: "To Finsbury Park." Asked about his cut fingers, Marwood agreed to make a written statement. He had been in a fight elsewhere, he said, and he knew nothing about an affray in Seven Sisters Road.

He and his fellow fugitive were released after further questioning, and if he had turned up for work as usual next day the police would probably not have suspected him. For no one had seen him wield the bloodstained knife – recovered from a pile of garden rubbish near the crime scene – which was identified as the murder weapon. But instead of reporting for work, he went into hiding, leaving Pentonville to stay secretly with friends in Chalk Farm.

Inevitably, his disappearance aroused suspicion. And within days his photograph was published in the newspapers, along with an announcement that he was wanted for further questioning in connection with the police constable's death.

Six weeks passed with no news of him. Then, around 7.15 p.m. on January 27th, 1959, he walked into Caledonian Road police station.

"I am Ronald Marwood," he told the desk sergeant. "I believe you are looking for me."

He wanted time to think, he said, when asked if he wished to make a statement. He had already made one mistake by going into hiding, and he was now about to make a second. Instead of asking for a solicitor, he spent the next three hours smoking cigarettes and drinking cups of tea while he pondered what he would say. No doubt he was recalling his father's words before he gave himself up: "Be straight. Tell them the truth."

He was said to have told Detective Superintendent Robert Fenwick: "You can write it all down. I did stab the copper that night. I will never know why I did it. I have been puzzling over in my mind during the last few weeks why I did it, but there just seems to be no answer."

Earlier in the evening of December 14th, the statement went on, someone had handed him a knife, telling him: "Here you are – you might need this."

When PC Summers began to lead Mike Bloom away, the statement continued: "I walked up behind the policeman, and as I got up to him he sort of half turned round and said words to the effect, 'Go away,' or 'Clear off.' He struck me with his fist in the region of my shoulder.

"I remember I had my hands in my overcoat pockets. I must have had my hand on the knife, which was in my right-hand pocket. I struck out with the intention of pushing him away. The policeman fell down. I stayed there for a few seconds. I felt dizzy. My head was spinning.

"There was never any intention on my part to use the knife. I must have been holding it in my hand when I pulled it out of my pocket to lash out at the copper.

"It wasn't until afterwards when I was running down

the road that I realised that it was still in my hand. That's about it. I would like to say that when I struck him I didn't realise the knife was in my hand."

His statement completed, he signed each page, initialled a correction, and finally wrote: "I have read this statement and it is true."

He was charged with murder and when he appeared before magistrates the next day his father was allowed to see him in a cell.

"Did you do it?" his father asked.

"Yes, Dad, I did" Marwood replied. "I told them the truth."

But, brought to trial at the Old Bailey the following month, he repudiated the statement in its entirety, pleaded not guilty, and declared that the statement was the opposite of what he actually said.

The court heard that 11 youths had been arrested and charged with involvement in the affray. Some had been sentenced and three would be called as witnesses.

The prosecutor, Mr. Christmas Humphreys QC, told the jury: "Constable Summers was fatally stabbed in the back while trying to prevent two gangs indulging in extremely bloody warfare. The evidence that the defendant was the person who stabbed – and the stabbing amounts to murder – comes from Marwood's statement and amounts, the Crown say, to very nearly a confession of murder. At least it is a confession that it was his hand that held the knife that killed the police officer."

He went on: "This most murderous weapon, ten inches long, was plunged deep and hard four or five inches into the policeman's body, which needs a real blow. Then Marwood runs, tells lies, comes to the police station, gives himself up and finally makes that statement which, in my submission, is the final item of evidence against him of knowing that he has wilfully murdered that police officer."

The first witness told the court that he was in Gray's dance hall that evening and left the premises at 10.40 p.m. He saw a crowd of youths fighting outside in the street. Three or four hatchets were "flying about" when a policeman walked into the fray and held a tall man. There was a scuffle and the officer staggered and fell to the ground.

Another witness said that when he saw the melee he walked down a side street and heard someone shout, "He has hit him!" He ran back to the corner and saw a policeman stumbling around and then falling.

Michael Bloom, who was serving a six-month prison sentence for his part in the affray, told the court that several "choppers" were being waved about. "I saw a police officer cross the road and everyone broke up. I started walking away. The policeman came up behind me and started nudging me up the road with his shoulder. Someone must have come along behind. I turned and heard him say, 'Clear off out of it.'

"He then said to me, 'Just a minute. I want to talk to you.' I believe he took hold of my arm for a second and then I heard a blow and I ran away."

He did not see who struck the blow, and added that everyone had had too much to drink.

A fourth witness who was in detention for his role in the fight said he fled with Marwood when the constable appeared. They jumped over several walls and he noticed that Marwood's hand was bleeding and that he held a handkerchief over it. Marwood told him that a chopper had cut him during the fight.

The court then heard that Marwood, the only son of an Islington fruit salesman, had won a scholarship to a grammar school, and his character was described as good when he completed his two years' National Service in the army. In 1956 he was convicted of shop-breaking, for which he was put on probation for two years. But he was generally regarded as quiet and well behaved.

The director of the Metropolitan Police laboratory, Mr. L. C. Nickolls, told the court he had made experiments with Marwood's overcoat with the knife in the right-hand pocket. He could not conceive of any way, he said, in which a man could have his hand in the pocket containing the knife and be unaware that it was there.

There were no fingerprints on the knife, the court was told. Fibres found on it had not come from Marwood's clothes and although his left hand was bleeding at the time of the stabbing, no blood was found on the constable's outer clothing.

In the witness-box Marwood said that on the night of the affray he met his friend Michael Bloom at the Spanish Patriots public house. After drinking about 10 half-pints of beer he got into a car with Bloom and three other men and they drove to the Double R Club in Bow Road. "Bloom and I were drinking rather heavily and I think I had another nine or ten half-pints of brown ale there."

Then they moved on by car to the dancing academy in Seven Sisters Road. "I just stood in the forecourt and I saw a group of people coming out of the dancing club," he said. "The next thing I remember was someone aiming a chopper at my head, and the blade hit my left hand, cutting two of my fingers. I felt a bit sick."

When he saw Bloom being held by a policeman he caught up with them. "As I got to the side of the policeman he turned round and said something like, 'Go away,' or 'Clear off.' As he said it he swung round with his left arm and caught me somewhere on the top of my left shoulder with the back of his fist. I rather lost my temper and punched him back. I used my right hand and aimed at his left shoulder, but I believe I hit him in the face. I realised afterwards I had hit him in the face."

"Did you have anything in your hand?" asked his counsel, Neil Lawson QC.

"No sir. I noticed he went back a bit. He staggered a bit. I took it that it was the force of my punch."

Instinctively he turned and ran. He said: "I realised I had done something wrong in hitting this policeman and I imagined he would be after me." He fled down a cul-de-sac and climbed over a wall into a garden, where he was joined shortly afterwards by the witness who had earlier told the court of their encounter.

Later that night, he went on, the two of them were

stopped by the police, to whom they told a false story. He was allowed to go home after making a statement but when he saw a newspaper report that the policeman had been stabbed in Seven Sisters Road he became scared. "I realised I had made a false statement to the police, which put me in rather a serious position, so I did not go back home. I thought it would be better if I stayed away for a while."

When he went to the police on January 27th, Marwood said, he was told that some of the youths arrested for making the affray had reported that he stabbed the constable.

"I denied it was me," he claimed, saying that when he made his statement the police "put down things I never said." He didn't read the statement, he told the court, and he was very tired when he signed it after being questioned for 10 hours. "I kept on insisting I never had a knife."

Cross-examining, Mr. Humphreys questioned him about his written statement to the police: "You say you had a knife in your right-hand coat pocket and pulled it out when you struck the officer, but did not realise you had the knife in your hand. I am suggesting that is nonsense. Would you like to put on the overcoat and try?"

"I did not have the knife in my overcoat pocket," Marwood replied.

"Do you understand the challenge I am putting to you?" the prosecutor persisted. "I am going to say it is impossible, and you might like the opportunity to put on the coat and have a wooden knife like the other, to see then if it is possible to have that knife in your pocket and not know it."

"I am not concerned with whether it is possible or not," Marwood countered, "because I did not have a knife."

"How drunk do you say you were at the time when I say you murdered that officer?"

"At the time when I hit the officer I was not very drunk, sir."

"Not very drunk but under the influence of drink?"

"Slightly under the influence of drink."

Mr. Humphreys next questioned Marwood about his disappearance after the fight. "You grew a moustache?" he asked.

"Yes sir."

"Let your hair grow long?"

"I didn't let it grow long."

"You didn't go out in the streets?"

"I did go out, sir."

"Very little?"

"Quite often."

"The pressure was growing on your friends and relations in the ever-increasing police inquiry, so in the end you were squeezed out of your hiding-place and gave yourself up?

"I wouldn't say I was squeezed out. I came out."

In his concluding speech for the defence, Mr. Lawson suggested that prisoners' statements should be tape-recorded to remove any doubt about what was said and by whom. There was hardly any evidence connecting Marwood with the stabbing, he said, apart from his second statement.

"I would suggest to you, members of the jury," Mr. Lawson continued, "that unless you are convinced that Marwood made his statement freely and voluntarily and that what he said in relation to his possession and use of the knife was actually true, then you should answer 'No' to the question, 'Did he strike the fatal blow?'

"If you think he might have struck the fatal blow in the confusion and excitement of the moment, meaning to push away the police officer, and if you come to the conclusion that at the moment the blow was struck his mental state was fuddled by drink and confused by the fighting in which he had been involved, then your verdict should be 'Guilty of manslaughter.'"

But if Marwood were telling the truth, the police were lying.

Dealing with his claim that his statement was doctored, Mr. Justice Gorman asked the jury in his summing-up:

A Brace Of Cop Killers

"How do you describe in mild terms the putting of this devilish concoction into the document? If you come to the conclusion that that statement substantially represents the truth and you are sure that there was a knife in the hands of the defendant that night, then it may help you to arrive at a view as to whether the prisoner did or did not strike the fatal blow."

On the fifth day of the trial the jury retired to deliberate for two hours and 42 minutes. They found Marwood guilty of capital murder and he was sentenced to death.

Repudiating his statement was Marwood's third fatal mistake. Had he stuck to that story, regardless of whether it were true or had been altered by the police, the jury might well have returned a manslaughter verdict, accepting the statement as a basically honest account.

Instead, the man alleged to have admitted the killing had added insult to injury by accusing the victim's colleagues of "putting down things" he didn't say. That could not have endeared him the jury, and they decided he was lying.

Were they wrong? Marwood was not the first defendant to disclaim an alleged confession and he would not be the last. His background made him an unlikely killer, suggesting that if he did indeed wield the knife that night this was in a moment of mental aberration.

It was not unknown, however, for the police to give perjured evidence. And in this case they had a strong motive: securing the conviction of a man suspected of killing one of their own.

But if Marwood were an unlikely killer, his story of a rigged confession was equally improbable. In addition to a superintendent, two senior officers were present when he made his statement, and the detective inspector who wrote it down testified: "I later told him he would be charged with murder and cautioned him. He replied: 'I have already told you the truth about how it happened in my statement.'"

And when the statement was read back to Marwood

85

the inspector said he insisted on the word "cut" being deleted and replaced by "hit" in a reference to his touching PC Summers.

So it seems he was not quite so tired when making his statement as he claimed.

Why did he repudiate it? Faced at the least with imprisonment for manslaughter it was surmised that he had decided to bid for an acquittal.

His appeal was dismissed, so his wife Rosalie, helped by two supportive priests, drew up a petition to save her husband. A reported 10,000 people signed the plea for clemency – and 150 Members of Parliament signed an appeal for his life on the basis that he was neither a habitual criminal, nor was the crime premeditated; that he had no link to the gang fight he was caught in; he was not in flight from another offence when the act was committed; and his statement to the police was disputed.

Home Secretary R. A. Butler received the petitions on May 1st, and on May 6th his decision was made public. Marwood would have to hang. Last-minute appeals to the Queen and the House of Lords came too late.

So in Pentonville Prison, almost within sight of his home, Ronald Marwood became the first man to be executed under the Homicide Act of 1957 for the murder of a police officer.

Ironically the considerable number of people who demonstrated outside the prison against the execution were believed to be motivated not by sympathy for the condemned man but by their dislike of the police. Their protest was noisy and threatening, and after the execution on May 8th, 1959, Harry Allen and his assistant executioner Harry Robinson slipped out of the prison via a back door that was then in use.

•

Two months after Harry Allen hanged Ronald Marwood, another police officer was shot dead in London. It happened in the ultra-smart block of flats at 105

Onslow Square in Kensington. To live there you had to be wealthy, so the last thing any of the residents expected to hear was a gunshot in the front hall of their luxury apartment block.

As they came running in alarm from their flats and peered over the staircase well, they saw a man lying in the corner of the hall. He was, they later discovered, Detective Sergeant Raymond William Purdy, who only four hours earlier had phoned his wife to say that he would be late home that evening.

Sergeant Purdy's killer was even then racing away from Onslow Square, hotly pursued by Purdy's colleague, Detective Sergeant John Sandford.

The two officers had been investigating blackmail calls to a Kensington resident, and a few minutes earlier had traced the caller to a phone box at South Kensington tube station. They watched the blackmailer, wearing dark glasses, leave the phone box, and followed him.

The man began to run, so the detectives gave chase. They caught him in nearby Onslow Square, outside No. 105, the block of flats, and took him into the building's entrance hall.

Detective Sergeant Sandford rang the porter's doorbell to ask him to make a phone call for a police car. There was no reply, and as Sandford turned back to his colleague the blackmailer pulled a gun from his pocket. The shot that brought the residents to their doors rang out, and Sergeant Purdy fell dying to the floor.

First on the scene was Mrs. Rositov, cook-housekeeper to Onslow Square resident Major John Waley. "There was nothing that could be done," she said. "First aid would have been useless." A Stock Exchange jobber, David Bruce, who lived in a ground-floor flat, dialled 999. "The detective remained unconscious for a few minutes, and then he died," said Mr. Bruce.

It was 3.30 p.m. on the afternoon of July 13th, 1959, a sweltering summer that year, when the manhunt for the cop-killer swung into action.

The first clues, clearly, would be provided by the woman being blackmailed. She was Mrs. Verne

Schiffman, and for two hours at Chelsea police station she told police how the previous week her apartment had been burgled. Among the stolen items were two passports. The mysterious blackmailer, almost certainly the burglar himself, was now demanding $500 for the return of the passports.

Mrs. Schiffman, a 30-year-old model, would have nothing to do with him. Instead, she phoned the police. "He spoke with a slight American accent," she recalled.

Three days later Chelsea Police knew the identity of the cop-killer, and his address – Room 15 at the Claremont House Hotel, in Queen's Gate, South Kensington. He was German-born Guenther Podola, and he was to make criminal history in Britain by pleading at his trial that he simply couldn't remember a thing about what happened.

Cautiously, a team of detectives approached Room 15, for Podola had a gun and had already killed with it. When they rang the bell there was no reply, although it later emerged that he was on the point of walking to the door to open it.

From the other side of the door the waiting detectives heard a click and, fearing the worst and without stopping to think more about it, 17-stone Detective Sergeant Albert Chambers threw himself at the door, which burst in under his weight.

He and another officer toppled into the room, and the door and the detectives fell on top of Podola, who was in fact unarmed, sending him sprawling. The blow knocked the German unconscious – and it was that blow, defence doctors were to claim, that caused Podola's total amnesia and prevented him from pleading to the murder charge.

When he recovered consciousness he was taken to the police station, where a doctor saw him before he was removed to St. Stephen's Hospital, Fulham. He was, said the doctor, bruised, scratched, dazed, frightened and exhausted. The doctor was also to say later that he could not establish mental contact with Podola, who

A relaxed Harry Allen. When Doris married him she had no idea he was a hangman

After reading an account of the hanging of Edith Thompson by John Ellis (above), Harry Allen resolved to become an executioner

Harry's diary entry recalling his first execution as a witness at Bedford Prison (below left). Below right, Harry out on the town in the 1940s

Alec de Antiquis lies mortally wounded in a London street. Christopher Geraghty and Charles Jenkins (bottom picture) were hanged for the murder

Five German P.O.W. Hanged For Murdering Comrade

FIVE German prisoners of war were hanged at Pentonville this morning for the murder of a fellow prisoner at a Pertha~~~~~~~~ ~~~~ December.

Announcement~~~~~~
hours earlier by th~~
Office.

The men were Kur~~
dorff, Erich Koenl~~
Marians Joachim G~~

Harry attended at the execution of five Germans on the gallows at Pentonville Prison

Christopher Craig,
Derek Bentley (right)
and below, hangman
Albert Pierrepoint.
Craig was too young
to hang, and Bentley
received a posthumous
Royal Pardon

Wandsworth Prison,
London, where your
author is a serving
prison officer

The gallows at Wandsworth Prison, rigged for testing with a weighted bag, and below, the position escorting officers took during an execution

The exterior of the gallows and condemned cell at the prison

Harry Allen's first execution as number one was the hanging of John Vickers (left) for the murder of Jane Duckett at her shop (below left) in Tait Street, Carlisle

Miss Duckett lies dead at the bottom of the cellar stairs

A jovial Harry at the bar of one of his pubs, and below, in uniform working for Singers

Robert Stewart. One of the last executioners

Scottish serial killer Peter Manuel. Above right, he leaves court en route to Barlinnie Prison and a date with Harry Allen, pictured below in bowler hat

was suffering "a withdrawal reaction to arrest."

Another doctor at the hospital found him to be "in a stuporous state." Since there were no physical injuries that could account for that, he concluded that the condition was consistent with a very severe mental shock.

Notwithstanding that, a week after the killing Podola was charged with the murder of Detective Sergeant Purdy. Thus the stage was set for a sensational trial that turned upon the question: was he feigning, or had he hit upon the best defence that could be thought up in the circumstances?

It was this issue that had first to be decided by a jury. The evidence that Podola was the murderer was overwhelming. What was in doubt was whether he was fit to plead, and that issue had to be decided by a separate, preliminary trial before the murder trial.

The trial on the fitness to plead began at the Old Bailey's famous No. 1 court with the case for the defence, for the judge ruled that it was Podola's duty to prove that he was unfit to plead. Although the British public was already seething at the idea that a cop-killer might get away with murder on such simplistic grounds, no one was quite ready for the opening submission by Mr. Frederick Lawton QC, defending. The presiding judge, Mr. Justice Edmund Davies, was to describe it as Podola's "unique claim" – for it had never before been entered as a defence to a murder charge.

Addressing the jury and speaking for his assisting counsel and for Podola's solicitors, Mr. Lawton said: "Although we appear for the prisoner, we have no idea what the defence is at all. We have no idea whether he wishes to say he was not there, no idea whether he wishes to say that witnesses for the prosecution are mistaken, inaccurate, or lying.

"We have no idea whether he wishes to say the gun was discharged accidentally, or whether he wishes to say he was provoked, and we have no information about his past. The reason is because he has been unable to give us any instructions, because he has lost his memory.

The consequence is that he is unable to defend himself against the charge of capital murder. Your sense of justice probably revolts at trying a man who cannot defend himself."

Podola, Mr. Lawton went on, had suffered concussion and this, together with a very severe fright, had probably caused his amnesia. After describing the circumstances of the arrest, he said: "I feel as a matter of fairness I should state specifically that there is no evidence of any kind that any violence was done to Podola at Chelsea police station. Indeed, such evidence that exists points the other way. His shock is the shock of his arrest and the circumstances of it.

"It is an easy thing to do to say you have lost your memory. Is it an easy thing to act it over a period of months?"

Defence witness Dr. John Shanahan, a police doctor, said that at the police station Podola was suffering from concussion. "His reaction was of not wanting to face up to reality."

Mr. Maxwell Turner, prosecuting, asked him: "Does it surprise you that a person should not want to face up to a charge of capital murder?'

"Not at all," replied the doctor.

Another medical witness, Dr. Philip Harvey, of St. Stephen's Hospital, said when he examined Podola no verbal communication was possible, and Podola did not appreciate the nature of spoken words. At a later examination he was far more conscious, but could say nothing and could understand nothing.

Mr. Lawton: "Silence can mean either conscious refusal to speak or inability to speak. Can you say what his silence meant?"

Dr. Harvey: "He wasn't silent, in the sense that he could make noises. They were the noises of a distressed person."

The judge: "Did he make exclamations, or what?"

Dr. Harvey: "They were occasional groans, my lord."

At yet another examination, Podola was refusing food and had fluid feeds. He gave the impression of wanting to be left alone. Days later his alertness greatly improved, but he wanted to know why he was in hospital.

Mr. Maurice Williams, a solicitor, was introduced to Podola in Dr. Harvey's presence, and he asked the prisoner whether he would agree to him acting as his legal adviser. "Podola appeared to me to be very puzzled," said Dr. Harvey.

Mr. Lawton: "Puzzled about what?"

Dr. Harvey: "He could not, I thought, recall any of the circumstances which were implicit in Mr. Williams' statement to him."

Among the doctors who came to the conclusion that Podola's loss of memory was genuine was Dr. Colin Edwards, who believed he was suffering from hysterical amnesia, triggered off by an injury to his head. Apart from that, he was sane and normal. What surprised Dr. Edwards, though, was that for a period of two months the hysterical amnesia extended over the whole of Podola's life. This was surprising because of its rarity.

The court was silent as Podola himself came into the witness-box. How would the jury react to him?

He told the court that he had three memories only, of a child called Mickey and a girl called Ruth, an incident where he found himself lying under a train, and of a whisper in his ear, a voice which he identified as Police Superintendent Hislop, saying, "I am your friend, say it was an accident."

Although he could recall nothing else of his life before July 17th, 1959, when he was arrested, he knew how to speak German, to play cards and chess. Asked how he knew these things, he said: "I just don't know."

He agreed he wrote a letter from prison to a man called Starkey, who had sent him a postcard. The letter, suggested the prosecution, clearly indicated that he knew Starkey, but that wasn't so, he replied. He wrote back to Starkey in cordial terms because this total stranger might send him some cigarettes and other comforts.

Four doctors called for the defence thought that his loss of memory was genuine. They were followed by the two prosecution doctors, who held that he was feigning. There had never been a genuine case of hysterical amnesia, said the prosecution doctors, covering a whole life, without symptoms which were absent in this case.

For nine days the jury listened to evidence on the submission that he had lost his memory. Now it was for them to decide. They retired for three and a half hours, and then returned to rule that he was sane and fit to stand trial on the murder charge.

A new jury was empanelled to try that charge. They heard the evidence of Detective Sergeant Sandford, the only witness to the shooting – evidence which, suggested Mr. Maxwell Turner, showed that the murder was the "deliberate act of a man determined to evade arrest."

For the defence, Mr. Lawton had to tell the new jury that he was in the "unique" situation for a barrister of having no instructions from his client on which to act. He could only suggest that they should consider whether the shooting was deliberate or an accident.

When the case for the prosecution ended, Podola rose in the dock and read a statement to the jury. Calmly he declared he could not put forward any defence. "I have lost my memory for all these events," he said. "I do not remember the circumstances leading up to the events in connection with this shooting. I do not know if it was me, or whether it was an accident or an act of self-defence.

"I do not know whether at that time I realised that the man was a detective. I do not know whether I was provoked in any way. For these reasons I am not able to admit or deny the charge against me."

The judge's summing-up task was much simpler than in the first trial. All the jury had to decide was whether the prosecution had proved that Podola shot Sergeant Purdy and that no one else could have done it. It took them only 38 minutes to come to the conclusion that he was guilty. When the black cap was placed on the judge's head, Mr. Justice Edmund Davies told him: "For that foul and terrible deed but one sentence is prescribed."

Then he sentenced the prisoner to hang. As he spoke, the cop-killer gripped the ledge of the dock with both hands and stared down into the well of the court, where the black automatic he had used to kill Sergeant Purdy lay on a table.

Guenther Fritz Podola's brief sojourn in England never took him out of London. He burgled in the capital, killed in the capital, was tried in the capital, and hanged in the capital, at Wandsworth Prison on November 5th, 1959. "It was my birthday," Harry Allen recalled. "I had to postpone the celebrations."

So who was Podola, the man who remembered nothing about himself? Quite a lot emerged in due course about his life, and what was evident was that there never was much hope for him. He was bound to end up in big trouble. For his outlook on life was convoluted, torn and self-destroying.

Even in the late 1950s the creed he clung to was outmoded: "I don't believe there is a God. He never does anything for me. Hitler was different. He was something tangible. He was a great man for Germany."

This was Podola – a wanderer through the world, lonely, lost and cynical. He was ardent and intelligent, but a fanatic for a lost cause. He loved fine music, he was a fluent letter-writer, but a killer.

He was born the son of a barber in Berlin in February, 1929. He was a year old when the family moved to a block of grey stone flats in the Alexander Platz in what was to become East Berlin. The square was called Red Alex because of the constant street battles between Communists, Nazis and police.

Neighbour Frau Anny Wegener remembered him as a boy with an imagination that was perhaps too vivid. "He was not very stable," she said. "Today he wanted this, tomorrow something else."

He was a good pupil at school, quick and above average intelligence. But he had no friends, and preferred doing his homework to going out.

Hitler's war smashed up the life of the quiet, happy family. Herr Werner Podola was called up, and Guenther, just 10 years old, joined the school group of the Hitler Youth.

Werner Podola was with the victorious Wehrmacht that smashed through France. The next year he was transferred to the Russian front. He was an infantry sergeant when he went into the battle of Stalingrad – and dead when he came out.

After the war Podola's mother returned from evacuation to Berlin. By that time her 16-year-old son had joined up and was missing, "somewhere in the East."

No one really knew what Podola was doing for the two years after the war, but almost certainly he was one of the hundreds of thousands of displaced people wandering around Europe at that time. When he came home to Berlin in 1947 he was hungry, tattered and bitter. He began to study music in the East Berlin music conservatory, where he met and fell in love with Ruth Quandt. She was a year younger and shared his interest in music.

It was her name that he whispered while lying dazed, bruised and handcuffed to a bed – and apparently suffering from amnesia – in Ward 5B of St. Stephen's Hospital, after his sensational arrest.

For the first two years that Ruth was his girl friend, Podola scraped along doing odd jobs. His mother insisted he find regular work, so he began to learn welding. Because it was a tough job, he had to give up his music studies.

His first boss was master welder Helmut Kaluza, who was still allowed by the Russians to keep his small private business. "Podola was a good chap, always punctual, intelligent and willing," he said.

In 1951 Ruth Quandt gave birth to baby Michael. But Podola had already decided to emigrate to Canada. "I'll come back to you and the baby when I've made good," he promised. Both then began to take English lessons.

He got his visa in 1952 and landed at Halifax, Nova Scotia, in August that year. Under the terms of his immigration agreement he was assigned to work on a 175-acre farm at Huntingdon, 50 miles south-east of

Montreal. For this he was paid $50 (then £17) a month and his keep.

Farm boss L. M. Kelly remembered him well. "He had a terrible temper. We all used to eat together in the farmhouse. Once one of my little girls playfully squirted her water pistol at him after lunch. He leapt up from the table. His face turned white. He clenched his fists and for a moment he seemed to lose his mind. I thought he was going to hit the child. Then one of the other fellows seized him by the shoulders, shook him and shouted at him to stop. He quietened as quickly as he became angry. After that I told the children never to tease the new German helper."

Podola left, as he was allowed to, a year after joining the farm. He joined the exclusive Mount Gabriel Country Club as an odd-job man and quit after only six weeks.

Tired of waiting for him back in Germany, Ruth Quandt married an American serviceman at Hanau, near Frankfurt. This seemed to increase his sense of hatred and bitterness.

He wrote to a German friend: "I don't really enjoy life, and become melancholy during my evenings and free hours. There are plenty of ways to entertain myself for cash, but once the excitement is over, loneliness is twice as hard to bear."

He found work as a welder, building Sabre jets for the Royal Canadian Air Force, and had jobs as a photographer, a labourer and a tailor. Then he wrote to his old welding boss, Herr Kaluza, in Berlin, about a new girl friend. "She is of French Canadian extraction and it seems her ancestors were high-born, as her name indicates. She's called Shayla de la Fontaine. She is my age and speaks English, French, Spanish, and enough German now to make herself understood.

"Her temperament and charm make her very popular among my friends and her own circle of admirers includes the West German consul. Her parents live in Ottawa. My prospective father-in-law has a garage of some size."

Ex-boss Herr Kaluza never heard from Podola again.

Later Podola met and dated Elsa Schmidt, a brunette from his native Berlin. But she soon gave him up. She said: "He used to frighten me with the way he talked. All about how he used to love the Hitler Youth movement. How life seemed very tame for him afterwards. There were rumours that he was going round with a fast crowd of hooligans. Then he started sending me expensive presents – mostly jewellery. I asked him where he was getting the money. I thought it over for a week or two and sent all his presents back. I never saw him again."

Elsa had guessed correctly where the money and the jewellery were coming from. In September, 1956, Podola was caught red-handed after breaking into a Montreal office block. Treated as a first offender, he was released into the care of a welfare association. He reported to them half a dozen times, and after that he didn't see them again.

Six months later he was caught driving a stolen car near Montreal. It was loaded with stolen property, two revolvers, a shotgun and a rifle. Found guilty of eight cases of housebreaking and two of theft, he was jailed for two years. He was released after 16 months and handed over to the captain of the *Seven Seas* for deportation to Germany.

For a time he worked as an unskilled labourer for a big metallurgical firm at Feuerbach in south Germany. Then the old wanderlust bug got him again and the lure this time was London. He got a three-month visa for Britain and left Düsseldorf airport on May 21st, 1959.

Podola discovered Soho, where the small-time crooks talked big, where the garish life of clubland and billiard bars enabled no-hopers to fill every waking moment. He stayed in two hotels and one guest-house, never remaining long enough to leave an impression behind.

He made two friends. One was clubland girl Norma Young. She called him Cinderella, because he always vanished from their dates at midnight. She thought he was "a perfect gentleman."

The other was a Soho hanger-on who used to eat in

cafes with Podola. He found him less attractive. He said: "He was a man filled with hatred."

Around the West End Podola was strictly third-rate. He was just another idler chasing the elusive fast buck that never came fast enough. He tried gambling. He tried all sorts of things, the most profitable of which seemed to be burglary. He had been in London only a few weeks when he burgled the Roland Gardens, South Kensington, flat of model Verne Schiffman, who was on holiday from America with her six-year-old daughter Lesley.

While Mrs. Schiffman was out, he broke in and stole jewellery and furs worth over £1,000, and the two passports over which he subsequently tried to blackmail her.

Acting on Mrs. Schiffman's complaint, the police listened into the phone conversations. Then came July 13th, the day when the blackmailer's voice kept talking to Mrs. Schiffman while the police moved in on the phone box at South Kensington tube station. A few minutes later Guenther Podola was a cop-killer.

CHAPTER 6

A BUSY YEAR ON THE GALLOWS

By the beginning of 1961 Harry Allen had hanged 15 men as chief executioner, a post he had held for four years. That year was to be the busiest year of his career – he would preside at seven hangings, and this at a time when only four more years remained before the abolition of capital punishment.

The first job of 1961 was the execution of Wasyl Gnypiuk in Lincoln Prison on January 22nd. Gnypiuk had murdered Louisa Surgey, 64, while burgling her home. The crime attracted little attention, and the hanging attracted hardly any at all. But the next two murder convictions were redolent with controversy.

The first concerned George Riley, whose story begins with a scene that can be witnessed any Friday. A small car drew up outside a suburban semi. A young man was at the wheel. It was payday, Friday October 7th, 1960, and he had come to call for his pal, who worked with him at the local butcher's shop, so that they could go out for a few pints together.

This was to become a night out with a difference – one that would be debated in Parliament, involve the Home Secretary, and be disputed for years to come.

Twenty-one-year-old George Riley had changed from his working clothes into his dark blue suit, white shirt and black suede shoes and was already waiting outside his home in Westlands Road, Shrewsbury, when his workmate drew up outside. By the end of their pub crawl Riley had knocked back 10 pints. But for him and his drinking buddy the night was still young. There was a dance on in the canteen at the town's Rolls-Royce factory, and the bar wouldn't close until 12.30 a.m.

By that time, Riley was to say later, he was more drunk than he had ever been in his life. All that beer had been topped up with probably as many as nine whiskies. He had also been involved in several fights, and when police were called they found him grappling with another youth on the canteen's red floor.

It was 1.30 a.m. when his pal drove him home and dropped him off in Westlands Road at his front gate. Half an hour later a neighbour just across the road was wakened by a violent scream. Deciding there was nothing to it, she turned over and went back to sleep.

One of George's brothers had to start work early, and he was having his breakfast at 5 a.m. when there was a knock at the window. George was outside and looking dishevelled. He said he had left his key in another coat pocket, and had spent the night on a settee in the garage. His forehead was grazed and his brother asked him if he had been in a fight. Yes, he had, he replied.

"Who won?"

"He did a bit and I did a bit," said George before going to bed. He was up again before seven and at work at eight, when his employer gave him a glass of fruit salts, thinking he looked off-colour.

That morning Mrs. Adeline Mary Smith, a 62-year-old widow, who lived across the road from George Riley's house, failed to answer her phone and police were called. They found her lying on her bedroom floor, her nightdress badly torn. She had been battered to death. Detective Inspector William Brumpton, at the crime scene, knew George Riley lived across the road, so he went across and knocked on the door. It was opened by one of Riley's brothers, the only person at home.

Brumpton went upstairs, opened Riley's wardrobe, and pulled out a crumpled blue jacket that appeared to be bloodstained. A search of the bedroom revealed shoes, socks and a pair of trousers, all liberally covered with mud.

The inspector set off for the butcher's shop where Riley worked. The suspect was to say later that he assumed the detective had come to question him about the dance hall brawl the previous night. But events moved with astonishing speed. Riley was taken to Shrewsbury police headquarters, questioned for the rest of the day, and at 7 p.m. he finished writing a statement in which he confessed to the murder of Adeline Smith.

He didn't know how long he had stayed on the settee in the garage, his confession said. Then it went on:

"But the next thing I recollect I was in Mrs. Smith's house, and I was after some money. I had spent more than I meant to that night, and knew she kept her handbag upstairs, because I have been to her for change and always saw her run upstairs for it.

"I got into the bedroom next to her bed and all of a sudden she jumped up and started shouting at me. I then grabbed hold of her by the nightdress and pulled her off the bed. It then tore down the front. I hit her in the face a couple of times to stop her from shouting because I was very frightened. She still continued shouting and grabbing hold of me to stop me running away.

"I then hit her once more and she let go of me and I ran out. She was still shouting as I run down the stairs. I got out the same way as I got in. I didn't take anything at all from the house. I was frightened. I ran over the fields. I didn't know in which direction and I didn't care as long as I got away.

"After I had been running for about ten minutes I stopped and found myself near the Grapes Inn. I then cut across the fields to my house, and went into the garage. I did not mean to hurt Mrs. Smith because I know her very well, and I only hit her because she jumped up and shouted and frightened me. I am very sorry things have ended like this. I didn't want to harm her. I only wanted some money."

So there it was – the suspect's admission of guilt, all written down in his own words. Everything seemed cut and dried, the outcome a foregone conclusion. But it wasn't. George Riley retracted his confession, the prosecution's only really hard evidence against him, for those stains on his suit turned out not to be blood but to have come from the red floor of the canteen where he had been seen struggling with another youth.

There were, it is true, specks of blood on his jacket

and trousers, but they were insufficient to match with the blood group of the victim and they could have been picked up during his scraps at the dance. And there were no stains at all on his shirt or tie, which, according to the evidence of the pathologist, should have been spattered with Mrs. Smith's blood.

Popular local feeling was very much hostile to Riley, and his lawyers made a successful application to have his trial moved from Shrewsbury to Stafford, where he appeared before Mr. Justice Barry on December 6th, 1960. He pleaded not guilty and it was soon evident that if he were to be convicted it would be solely on his own now-disputed confession.

The pathologist, Dr. E. G. Evans, told the court that Mrs. Smith was killed by about half a dozen heavy blows to the face from a fist which had worn a ring like George Riley's. But examination of Riley's ring, taken from him shortly after his arrest, revealed only a tiny speck of blood too small to be identified – blood which, again, could have been acquired during a fight at the dance.

Scrapings had been taken from beneath the victim's fingernails in the hope that they might contain fragments of the skin Riley had lost when his forehead was grazed, but nothing incriminating was found. A footprint discovered in Mrs. Smith's front garden did not correspond with Riley's shoes, and there were no fingerprints.

A weakness in the prosecution's case sprang from the fact that Mrs. Smith's purse was in a drawer of her dressing table, apparently untouched. The prosecution needed to prove that something was stolen if they wanted to pursue a case of murder in the furtherance of theft in order to establish the crime as a capital offence. The untouched purse did nothing for their case.

Mr. Justice Barry told the jury that if they chose to disregard Riley's statement as a confession, "then the prosecution do not invite you to say that all the remaining evidence is sufficient to convict this man of this very serious offence."

Riley did not deny having made the statement – he

could not disown it since it was in his own handwriting – but he claimed he wrote it under what amounted to duress. He was so drunk that night that he simply couldn't remember what he had done after he returned home. And when the police told him they had ample evidence of his guilt, and gave instances, he thought they must be right.

He said that while he was being questioned officers kept coming into the room with slips of paper for the inspector who, upon reading them, would announce the discovery of yet another item of evidence against him. Finally, on being handed the last piece of paper, Brumpton said: "Prepare yourself for a shock – the woman is dead!" This of course was something the police had known all along.

Inspector Brumpton later explained to the court why he did not inform Riley of Mrs Smith's death from the outset. He admitted that in the initial stages of the investigation he wanted to divulge as little as possible.

Riley claimed that Brumpton told him his footprint was found in Mrs Smith's garden, that his fingerprints were in her house and the clothes he was wearing, now in the possession of the police, were heavily bloodstained. And as these "facts" were repeatedly put to him he believed them, having no clear recollection of his own.

He was feeling ill, doubtless due to a hangover from his binge the night before and his lack of sleep. So the constant questioning and reiteration of the apparent evidence against him had simply worn him down. Detective Inspector Brumpton left the office at one point, leaving him alone with Detective Sergeant Norman Phillips. They chatted together, but Phillips kept bringing the conversation back to Mrs. Smith's death and the need for him to make a statement.

At last, when the sergeant said, "Come on, you did it, didn't you? Didn't you?" he replied, "Yes."

Riley told the court that the sergeant then asked him, "How did you do it?" and he replied, "I did it like the D.I. said."

"Good, you can make a statement now," the sergeant told him, adding that this would make things easier for him.

What were his thoughts as he wrote down the confession? "I thought it would help me," he told the court. "I knew I would remain a prisoner, but I thought they would – you know, stop...leave me alone." While he was writing the inspector returned, took a look at it and asked, "Were you going up for money?"

Riley replied that he was, whereupon Brumpton told him: "Well, go on then, put that down." So he wrote that he knew Mrs. Smith had lots of money and kept her handbag upstairs.

That was Riley's story. But the detectives' account was somewhat different. Brumpton and Phillips denied telling their prisoner about fingerprints or bloodstains, and they denied pressing him to confess.

Phillips told the court that Riley and himself exchanged no words while they were alone together for 90 minutes. While Riley sat at a desk, the sergeant occupied himself with other work. Mr. Ryder Richardson QC, defending, asked: "Not a word passed between you?"

"No."

"He never asked when he was going to be let go?"

"No."

"Or what you were holding him there for?"

"No."

"Or whether he was charged?"

"No."

"He never at any time asked for his solicitor?"

"He did not."

"Or his father?"

"No, sir."

Phillips said the silence was broken only when Riley at last asked: "They top you for capital murder, don't they?" And then, following a discussion about the meaning of capital murder, Riley said: "She was alive when I left her. I wanted some money. I can't remember everything. I was drunk."

When his counsel asked him why he said Mrs. Smith

was alive when he left her, he replied: "I just did not like the thought of killing anyone and leaving anyone dead on the floor." He did not deny having made the remark.

After a little less than two hours' deliberation the jury returned with their verdict. They found Riley guilty, and he was sentenced to death. His subsequent appeal was dismissed, but his story was far from over.

An anonymous letter outlining his plight was sent from Shrewsbury to a noted opponent of capital punishment. The recipient contacted Leon Blom-Cooper, at that time legal correspondent of the *Observer* newspaper. Blom-Cooper went to Shrewsbury and two days later, on Sunday, February 5th, under the heading "Another Evans Case?," his newspaper reported:

"A handful of Salopians feel that in George Riley, a 21-year-old butcher's assistant, due to be executed in the local gaol on Thursday (unless a reprieve intervenes) they have a condemned man whose case bears in two vital respects a striking resemblance to the fate of Timothy Evans."

The Evans case of 1950 was still fresh in readers' minds. He was convicted and hanged on the evidence of a confession he retracted, and it was now suspected that there was a miscarriage of justice.

In 1966, on the advice of the Home Secretary, Evans was granted a posthumous pardon by the Queen after a High Court judge found that he was "probably innocent" of the murder of his wife and daughter at 10 Rillington Place, the house occupied by the multiple murderer John Christie, who followed Evans to the gallows in 1953.

Blom-Cooper's report went on to point out that Riley was convicted "almost entirely on his own confession made, moreover, to the police after he had been in custody for some seven hours. Almost no other evidence which could remotely be called corroborative was produced to substantiate Riley's statement that he had intended to rob a widow and, in a panic, brutally murdered her."

The report also recalled how at Riley's trial Professor J. M. Webster, the defence pathologist, said that the condition of Mrs. Smith's face indicated that blood must have spurted all over her attacker, and the force of the blows must have been considerable.

Yet there were only a few spots of blood on Riley's jacket, possibly resulting from a dance hall brawl, Blom-Cooper continued, and no evidence was produced that Riley's knuckles were lacerated. The report asked if the police were over-zealous in obtaining the confession, which Riley claimed was made with suggestive promptings from Detective Inspector Brumpton.

"Certainly they were well content with relying on it once it had been made...but having made a watertight case for the prosecution within 12 hours of the crime having been discovered, the police rested content and made no further investigation which might have suggested an alternative culprit."

Blom-Cooper contended that the Homicide Act of 1957 had been intended "to retain the death penalty for professional criminals, those who habitually rob with violence. It was not intended to catch in its expansive net the murderer who committed the crime in the course of a technical theft. And Riley's 'theft' was not only technical, but could be proved in evidence only by admitting his own statement to the police."

There was also another disquieting aspect of the trial. When the jury retired the judge instructed that they take with them horrific photographs of Mrs. Smith's murdered face. This was surely more likely to prompt an emotive verdict than a reasoned one.

And something else may have been stacked against Riley in the jury's minds. No mention had been made of his criminal record, but it was probably known to some of them because his last escapade had made headlines.

He was charged with attempted murder after stabbing two teenagers with a flick-knife during a drunken brawl. When the charge was reduced he received a nine-month prison sentence for wounding with intent to cause grievous bodily harm. That had been less than two years ago. Riley also collected two theft convictions when he was 14.

All this explained why Detective Inspector Brumpton had so promptly popped across the road from the murder scene to knock at Riley's door. The detective knew where he lived and knew he had form, for Brumpton himself had led the stabbing investigation.

Unknown to the jury, however, there were also muddy waters on the prosecution's side. Detective Inspector Brumpton had recently been suspended from duty while an inquiry was conducted into allegations that he had tampered with evidence in another case. Although he was cleared, there were inevitable suspicions of a whitewash.

This, together with other factors, was brought to the attention of R. A. Butler, the Home Secretary, when the *Observer* report stirred MPs into action. The day after Blom-Cooper's report from Shrewsbury appeared, a question was put down on the Order Paper of the House of Commons seeking an inquiry into whether there was a miscarriage of justice. This was raised by Sydney Silverman, a noted abolitionist, and together with two other Labour MPs he called on Mr. Butler.

The Home Secretary promised that he would consider all they had told him, saying he would take the information they had given him home that evening together with other relevant papers to give the case his full attention. But the next morning Riley's solicitor, Tony Hayes, received a letter in the first post informing him there would be no reprieve. This suggested that the Home Secretary had already made up his mind when he received the delegation.

Butler could still have changed his decision, but he didn't. Tony Hayes petitioned the Queen, to no avail. He last saw Riley on the eve of the execution. "There was no confession or anything like that," he said. "He just shook my hand and thanked me for all I had done. He was much calmer than I was."

George Riley's three brothers also visited him. "George, did you do it or not?" asked the eldest.

"No, I didn't" Riley replied. He had earlier told his father not to worry and not to forget him.

As Harry Allen settled into bed in Shrewsbury Prison that night, in preparation for the next morning's hanging, residents of streets around the prison were having a disturbed sleep. The gaol's windows were rattled and doors inside were banged repeatedly as prisoners chanted, "Don't let George hang!" and "Don't hang Riley!"

"I have never head anything like it," one woman told a reporter. "The horror of all it meant was sickening."

At eight o'clock on February 9th, 1961, Harry strode into the death cell, together with his assistant Samuel Plant, and led Riley to the scaffold. Harry made no comment on the controversial execution, but his colleague, executioner Syd Dernley, had plenty to say.

Dernley went to Shrewsbury on November 10th, 1989 – 28 years after Riley's execution – on a publicity tour for the launch of his book, *The Hangman's Tale*. He had not of course been involved in Riley's hanging, and that perhaps was just as well, for there were still those around who thought the whole thing was a travesty. One of them was a newspaper photographer who buttonholed the retired executioner.

He was Bob Carter, of the *Shropshire Star*, and he had covered the crowd scenes outside Staffordshire Assize Court when George Riley was on trial. Carter was a friend of Riley's, and the photographer was convinced of his innocence.

Telling friends that Riley had broken up more fights than he had started, Carter wasn't alone in thinking that someone else killed Mrs. Smith, adding that they all had a good idea who the real culprit was. And Riley's solicitor suspected that his client knew who had actually committed the crime for which he paid with his life.

Syd Dernley thought long and hard about what Bob Carter told him. "You might not think that I should have a conscience, but I do, although it is very small," he said. "In my opinion Riley's trial was a botched-up job. It seems to me that the prosecution were too keen and anxious to convict, and that the judge could have directed the jury more thoroughly. Riley should have been reprieved because of the lack of confirmative evidence.

"I'm glad I wasn't on the job."

Plenty of people felt like Bob Carter. Despite Riley's troubled past he was popular and his friends said that although he was never one to shirk a scrap, he was better known for intervening to separate brawlers, or for going to the assistance of his mates, than for starting fights. He was a schoolmaster's son, and the butcher who employed him liked him and trusted him with the key to his shop, where the safe contained anything up to £200.

Others, however, bayed for Riley's blood, appalled by the elderly widow's brutal murder and believing him guilty. Blom-Cooper thought they were in the majority. The *Observer* report raised questions never satisfactorily explained away. On Mrs. Smith's staircase, Blom-Cooper noted, "there were two separate pieces of blood-bespattered wallpaper which the police removed. The widow's assailant obviously left her dying in the bedroom and brushed his bloodstained jacket on the staircase wall as he descended. Yet these two vital pieces of evidence were missing at the trial.

"Was it that the pathological test on those two pieces of wallpaper did not fit in with the police theory of the crime, just as the time-sheets of the workmen in the wash-house of 10 Rillington Place were never available at the trial of Timothy Evans?"

But as Blom-Cooper pointed out, the police were not obliged to produce evidence that didn't assist the prosecution.

During the course of a historic debate on the case in the House of Commons, bitter allegations were made against the police for irregularities in their evidence. One of the most telling questions raised was: if George Riley was the killer, why was there only a speck or two of blood on his clothes? That was something his solicitor could never understand. Neither could the pathologists. It baffled everyone.

For a different jury, a panel not shut away with emotive pictures of the victim's gory face for company, the virtual absence of blood on the accused man's clothes might have constituted "reasonable doubt." But George Riley wasn't given that benefit; like Timothy Evans, when he signed his confession he signed his own death warrant.

There were two other ironies. Had Riley been tried in Scotland he would have been acquitted, for north of the border no one could be convicted on the basis of a confession alone. So thin was the rest of the case against him that he probably wouldn't even have gone to trial.

As for Mrs. Smith's "lots of money" to which he referred in his confession – had her purse been stolen the thief would have been richer by 18p. It contained three shillings and sevenpence ha'penny.

•

Seven weeks after hanging George Riley, Harry was assigned to his third execution of that year. The victim, Jack Day, was a bit of a tearaway like George Riley. But he was contrite in the end. He told Harry as the noose was put round his neck: "I'm sorry I did it. I didn't really want to kill him."

Weaponry was Jack Day's passion. Before he was arrested for murder he had recently disposed of his collection of 177 firearms and swords, but he still had his cherished .38 Enfield revolver. On the evening of August 23rd, 1960, he took the gun with him to the Horse and Jockey pub at Kensworth, near Dunstable, and entertained fellow-customers with a demonstration of Russian roulette.

Foolhardy? Well, yes. But those who knew the 30-year-old car salesman were not surprised. A former dirt-track rider, he had long had a daredevil reputation and the roulette demonstration was entirely in character. His friends smiled as they watched, unaware that the police would soon be urgently seeking that revolver

– and not just because it was unlicensed.

Two days later Tony Sinfield was baling hay in one of his meadows on Dunstable downs, when he noticed a man's jacket lying in nettles near an outhouse. Taking a closer look, he spotted a shoe protruding from behind some sacks. Stopping to pick up the shoe he found it contained a foot. He pulled the sacks aside to reveal the body of a man lying on his back.

Police were quickly on the scene, and documents in the man's pockets identified him as Keith Godfrey Arthur, a 25-year-old machine operator employed at a local factory. He was also a second-hand car dealer, and lived in Dunstable's Morcom Road with his wife and two children.

He had died, said the Home Office pathologist Dr. Francis Camps, from a single gunshot wound, and had been killed elsewhere.

Detective Superintendent Dennis Hawkins, called in from Scotland Yard to lead the inquiry, decided that because the body was found in an outhouse hidden from the road by thick hedgerows, the killer must be a local man, and "elsewhere" must be somewhere in the Dunstable area.

Dozens of police officers searched the vicinity of the crime scene for the murder weapon, but they couldn't find it. Convinced that the killer was somewhere in the town, Hawkins put every officer in Dunstable on the alert, with orders to report anything suspicious. He could only hope that something would turn up – and soon something did, but in a way he could never have imagined.

"Blood!" cried a young policewoman, pointing excitedly to a red trail that ran down a Dunstable street. Her companion, Detective Sergeant George Slater, clicked the shutter of his camera repeatedly as they followed the red spots along the pavement.

They led to a house in Edward Street, and the policewoman knocked on the door. It was opened by a young woman, who said she was Mrs. Dowling, and she didn't live there. She was looking after the house for the owner, a friend who was out shopping.

"Can you explain this blood on the doorstep?" the policewoman asked her.

"Oh, that isn't blood," Mrs. Dowling laughed. "It's red paint. There was a rather careless painter here this morning. But don't go away. I think perhaps you should come round to my house in Periwinkle Lane and talk to my 13-year-old daughter Pat. She told me before she went to school this morning that she thinks she recently witnessed a murder."

The schoolgirl's story was almost as bizarre as the red trail of paint. She was, she said, a regular baby-sitter for Jack Day and his wife Margaret, who lived nearby in Edward Street. On August 23rd she was at their house when Mrs. Day came home soon after 8 p.m. and asked her to pop out and buy a frozen pork pie.

She did so, Pat continued, and when she came back about 10 minutes later Mrs. Day had a visitor, a man she subsequently learned was Keith Arthur. She remembered him looking at her and saying something about a pendant she was wearing, and then they talked about a bracelet on his wrist. He said every link was nine carat gold, and Mrs. Day didn't believe him.

They were still talking about the bracelet, Pat said, when Mr. Day came into the house through the back door. Mrs. Day was sitting down and Mr. Arthur was standing near her.

"What are you doing here?" Mr. Day asked him.

"The way he said it," Pat recalled, "I thought they were going to fight or something. Then Mr. Arthur said, 'I came to see if you would buy me a drink,' or something like that.

"Mr. Day then said, 'This will go with it,' or something similar, and pulled a gun from his pocket. I heard a bang and saw a flash, and then I ran home."

Jack Day had once been reported as owning a .38 Enfield revolver for which he was not registered, but the police had been unable to find it.

The investigators learned that he had been heard to say he would shoot anyone who had an affair with his wife. They also learned that Keith Arthur had often bragged about his affairs with women.

On August 26th, the day after Arthur's body was found, Jack Day was arrested at the Horse and Jockey. Blood on his clothes was found to be of the same group as Keith Arthur's, and soil and debris on his trousers matched samples taken at the farm outhouse where the corpse had been hidden. And in the storeroom of the garage where Day worked, police found his .38 Enfield revolver.

It seemed an open-and shut case, until he made a statement.

"I came home from the Horse and Jockey, parked my car and went indoors," he said. "Keith was there. I hadn't seen him for some time. I said 'Hello' to him, like you know. I went to take off my clothes as I got indoors. The wife and the baby-sitter were there. That is why I cannot understand how it happened. I took my gun out of my pocket. It was in a handkerchief.

"I put the gun down on the settee. The next thing I knew, the damned thing went off. Keith was standing there. I said, 'Blimey, sorry it happened.' He said, 'It has got me in the throat.'

"He looked as if he had been scratched like, everything happened quick. I gave him my handkerchief to put on it. I had two handkerchiefs, one on the gun and another in my pocket."

Day then claimed that he and Arthur, who was bleeding heavily, went into Dunstable town centre and looked in vain for help. "We went to see if we could find a doctor down the town. We got as far as the milk bar and Keith collapsed. No one came to give us a hand, but he was choking, you know, and coughing blood out of his mouth.

"I got my arm around him and we rushed home. I ran all the way down to the square to get my car – that's the square near the public conveniences. When I got back home Keith was lying in a pool of blood in the kitchen. I picked him up and took him through the house to put him in the car.

"He was dead when I got him into the car. I just panicked and I didn't know what to do. I don't know how I got him into the car. I didn't know what to do with him, so I dropped him in that old shed up the top there.

"I just grabbed any old thing to cover him. I knew they would find him. It was dark. I expected to find you when I got back. The wife told me to give myself up, but I daren't. That is the truth.

"I wrapped the gun up the following day, and the ammunition I got with it. You can go and pick it up now. I knew you must find out anyway. It's in the spares building at Stansbridge Motors."

The police learned that Day was familiar with the farm outhouse where he dumped the body, because he was related to the Sinfields.

At his trial at Bedfordshire Assizes in January, 1961, firearms experts testified that Keith Arthur was shot at a range of not more than nine inches. A defence expert agreed with the prosecution expert that the gun was in good working order and that a pressure of 14 lbs on the trigger was required to fire it. They agreed, too, that it could not fire accidentally. "The Enfield .38 is the safest revolver in the world," said one of the experts, Ralph Murray.

Denying murder, Day told the court that he had the day off on August 23rd. He went out for a drink at lunchtime, and then went to a cinema and afterwards to the Horse and Jockey. Throughout this time the revolver, fully loaded, was in his pocket. He carried it around with him because his wife didn't like guns to be left in the house, and he usually kept it in his car's door pocket.

The regulars at the Horse and Jockey knew of his interest in guns, and the talk turned to tricks played with them. Russian roulette was discussed, and one of the drinkers bet him £1 that he couldn't play it.

"I demonstrated how to do it, and how safe it is to do it," Day said, explaining that he showed his saloon bar audience that if one bullet were put in the chamber of a revolver and the chamber was spun, the weight of the single bullet would ensure it would come to rest at the chamber's bottom. Pulling the trigger after the spin stopped would therefore be perfectly safe.

Day then showed the jury how he had wrapped his handkerchief around the gun before placing it tightly in his pocket and leaving the pub after a few drinks. As he stepped outside, he said, he saw the police waiting. "I knew they were trying to catch me on a drink-driving charge. It annoyed me."

He drove home, still feeling angry and thinking of going to the police station to complain that in the last two months they had been outside the pub every time he came out after a drink. He had reported this once before, and the police had said they knew nothing about it.

On arriving home on the evening of the shooting, he saw the baby-sitter was in the living-room, standing near the door. He wasn't sure what he said to Arthur, but he thought it was something like, "How are you?"

Asked by Mr. C. W. Abrahams, defending, if he had asked Arthur, "What are you doing here?" Day replied, "It may be perfectly true, sir, I may have said that."

He remembered Arthur saying, "I've come to see if you'll buy me a drink, Jack," and he replied. "It depends what you want to go with it." This was a standing joke between them, Day said. It indicated whether he could afford to buy a chaser, and Arthur would know by the remark how he was "fixed." When he drank a glass of beer, Day explained, he followed it with a glass of spirits whenever he could.

He said that on entering the living-room he began to unbutton his coat. "I pulled the handkerchief with the gun in it from my pocket. As I pulled the handkerchief off the gun it went off, I don't know how or why. I wasn't looking at Keith when the gun went off. To my knowledge I didn't touch the trigger."

He recalled that after the shot the baby-sitter was standing near the door with her hands over her ears. His wife was sitting in a chair and "her mouth dropped open." Out of the corner of his eye he saw Arthur spin round.

"I think I said, 'Sorry,' or something like that," Day went on. According to his account, Arthur shook his right hand, and put his other hand to his shirt, saying, "It got me through the shirt," before walking across the room and sitting down. When he took his hand away there was hardly a mark. "It just grazed you," Day told him.

Arthur then moved to get a handkerchief out of his pocket, but before he could find it blood started coming through his fingers. "We'd better go to the doctor's," Day told him, and they went out together and began to walk to Dr. Pinkerton's surgery.

Because it was dark, Day told the court, he couldn't see how badly Arthur was injured until they reached a zebra crossing in the High Street. Then Arthur collapsed on the ground beside him.

"He was in a terrible state," Day continued. "There was blood all over the pavement. I was really worried by this time. I picked him up and said, 'Come on, Keith, we'll go down to the hospital.'"

He told Arthur to wait there while he ran back to fetch his car. By this time Arthur was choking on his own blood.

Day said he put his arm round Arthur's shoulder and helped him along Regent Street, half-carrying, half-dragging him. Arthur could hardly walk, and fell down a couple of times. Day finally got his car and got him into it, but as they were setting out for the hospital Arthur fell forward on the car's floor.

"I saw his face then," Day said. "I realised he was dead. I think it was then that I went to pieces. It's a job to explain what I did next. I wanted to get rid of him, but I didn't want to. I think that's why I went up to the farm outhouse, because I thought someone would find him up there. I don't remember much about the ride, but I remember opening the door and picking him up. He fell from my hands on to the ground. I think I fell over him trying to pick him up."

He dragged Arthur to the outhouse. It was pitch dark there, but he knew the layout because he used to go to the outhouse when he was out shooting.

"I seemed to go mad," he said. "I just dragged everything all over the place."

When he arrived home again his wife asked, "How's Keith?" He replied. "He's dead."

His wife gave him the bullet, and he was surprised to see it was almost undamaged. He put it and the cartridge case together and put them in his pocket. His gun, he said, was a safe one, and with such a firearm a careful person would cause no damage.

Asked why he didn't take Arthur to the ambulance station, he replied: "I knew there was no one there. At least, I have never seen anyone there. It is always dark at night."

Cross-examined, he said he used to practise shooting in a field with a revolver strapped to his side. He liked to see how fast he could draw it. "It's a hobby with me. Some people take up golf. I took up guns."

He would shoot pigeons perched on walls through his car windows, he said, and he once killed a fox with a .45 revolver.

The judge asked: "Are you telling the jury that in case you saw a pigeon on a wall you carried a revolver to shoot out of the car window?"

"Yes," Day replied.

"What about people on the other side of the street?"

"I mean in the country."

He was not jealous about his wife, he said. Told that he had been heard to say he would shoot anyone he caught with her, he said, "I don't remember having made such a remark. It isn't the type of remark I make."

Day complained about the way he was arrested in the Horse and Jockey. The police, he said, came in "like a fire engine." One officer gripped his left arm, another his right arm, and a third ran his hands all over him.

"They came through the door in a rush. One pulled my wallet out of my pocket. Everyone was standing there and staring. The only thing that gets my back up is when I have any dealings with the police. I once told them that any time they thought I was intoxicated I would take them from A to B in perfect safety in a car."

Dr. Rowland Hill said that after examining Day he concluded that he had never been capable of leading a life of steady, methodical and progressive routine, with a normal sense of serious purpose. "I found him lacking in normal balance, sense of proportion and responsibility."

The hushed court then watched Margaret Day go hatless, and wearing a fur coat, into the witness-box. She had no feelings for Keith Arthur, she said. She didn't like him and thought nothing of him, but she thought he was a person who might like her.

Before the night of the shooting he had never been to her home in her husband's absence, and he was there only a minute before the baby-sitter returned from running an errand.

Asked if her husband was jealous about her, she said he was possessive. She had never tried to make him jealous or maintain his interest by pretending she had been out with other people. On the night of the shooting she said her husband spoke first to Arthur. "He said, 'What are you doing here?' although I don't think they were his exact words. It wasn't in an angry voice, and I didn't sense there was trouble in his tone.

"Keith said he had come to see if Jack would buy him a drink. Jack made some remark back to him. I believe he said, 'You have come after my wife.' It did sound then as if there might be trouble."

At this point Mrs. Day broke down and sobbed, but quickly recovered.

When the gun went off, she said, Arthur went to his knees. "Jack said to Keith, 'Get up and don't be silly.' Keith was supported by my husband out of the house. My husband was dragging him by the feet. I was in the house when they came back. They were gone about seven or eight minutes. They came to the back door. My husband said he was going to get his car to take Keith to the hospital. Keith at this time was on the kitchen floor.

"I looked round the living-room and found a bullet under the table. One of the walls was grazed, so I put an extra piece of wallpaper of the same pattern over the mark.

"My husband came back at about ten-fifteen. I asked him where Keith was. At that time I didn't know he was dead. My husband replied, 'I have just dug his grave.' I told him to go to the police. After that we had no further conversation about it."

An earlier witness had testified that Mrs. Day had told her she used to make her husband jealous by dressing up to look as if she had been out. Asked about this, Mrs. Day said she had never said anything of the sort. She couldn't recall her husband threatening to shoot anyone he found with her, but he might have done.

When the gun discharged she did not notice a handkerchief, nor did she find one in the room afterwards. At the sound of the shot she panicked and ran into the hall.

The baby-sitter, Patricia Dowling, saw no handkerchief around the gun either. When Jack Day spoke to Arthur, she testified, he didn't sound very happy.

In his final speech for the prosecution, Mr. John Hobson, QC, MP, said Day shot Arthur in a temper, and two things made his story unacceptable. The first was that the revolver could not go off accidentally. A handkerchief might pull back the cocking piece, but the gun would not fire unless the necessary pressure was placed on the trigger.

There was also the evidence that Arthur's throat wound was caused by a weapon discharged at a distance of no more than nine inches, and Day had said nothing about being that close.

"Perhaps a test of his veracity may be made about the point whether he pulled Arthur from the house with his arms under Arthur's armpits. Mrs. Day says he was dragged out by the feet."

For the defence, Mr. Arthur James QC said Day was a

man who had never grown up. He carried a gun not for any offensive purpose but because, as one witness put it, a gun was part of him.

"He is not a jealous man, as has been suggested, except, perhaps, in the sense that he is very fond of his wife and three children. Some men are rather more possessive than others and that might be termed an aspect of jealousy."

There were two accounts of what had happened, Mr. James said. There was the baby-sitter's evidence and what Day had said in his statement. At one stage the prosecution had seemed to be setting out to show that the baby-sitter had seen the gun withdrawn from Day's pocket without a handkerchief covering it, but her testimony fell far short of that. She had only said, "I can't remember back over five months. I wasn't particularly interested in what people were doing or saying, but heard certain words spoken."

She had heard Day ask Arthur what he was doing there in a tone that she thought was angry, and she edged towards the door.

"That is the evidence of the prosecution," Mr. James told the jury. "But are you to determine this matter on the evidence of one young girl as to her interpretation of the tone of this man's voice?"

Throughout the trial Day maintained an air of disinterest, at one point laughing. "I hope you will treat this case seriously," the judge told him. "There is nothing whatever to laugh at."

It took the all-male jury only 20 minutes to decide that Day was guilty of murder. Asked if he had anything to say, he replied, "No, only that I am not guilty, sir. I didn't pull the trigger." Mr. Justice Streatfeild then sentenced him to death.

From the public gallery Day's mother shouted: "You have sentenced an innocent man! You will regret it!" She was dragged screaming from the court, and then fainted.

After the trial it emerged that although a medical expert had concluded that Day was a psychopath, the killer had rejected his counsel's advice to plead guilty on the ground of diminished responsibility.

He refused to appeal until the seriousness of his situation finally dawned upon him. Then his appeal was dismissed, and his appointment with Harry Allen on the scaffold was fixed for March 29th, 1961. As he languished in the death cell, there was a bizarre twist to his final days on Earth.

Three days before the execution *The Spectator* published a letter that said that Day had been convicted and hanged. His lawyers promptly sued, claiming that the letter was libellous because it suggested that his crime was so heinous that he had no hope of a reprieve.

Next day he was told that the Home Secretary had decided against clemency, and Day's legal action died with him on the scaffold.

Because of his daredevil lifestyle, Jack Day had often bragged that he would not live beyond 30. Now he was proved right. For that was his age when Harry Allen placed the noose around his neck and pulled the lever to open the trap-doors that plunged him to his death.

CHAPTER 7

THE BUSIEST YEAR – CONTINUED

Two months after hanging Jack Day at Bedford Prison, Harry Allen's busiest ever year – 1961 – continued with the execution at Wandsworth of a young bank robber.

The date that Victor Terry chose to rob a bank and commit capital murder, November 10th, 1960, had a particular significance, because minutes earlier on that very same day his friend Francis Forsyth had just been hanged at Wandsworth by Harry Allen.

Forsyth was executed for his part in the murder of Allan Jee, who was kicked to death and robbed of the contents of his pockets. He was the last 18-year-old to be executed.

That same morning, while Forsyth's body was still in the post-mortem room adjacent to the Wandsworth Prison scaffold, his friend Victor Terry drove up with another friend to a bank. This was Lloyds' new branch in Field Place, a shopping centre in Durrington, near Worthing.

Five minutes earlier, 61-year-old bank guard John Henry Pull, together with a cashier, had arrived to open the bank. After they let themselves in, the cashier opened the vault and took out an attaché case containing money collected from the tills the previous afternoon. He put the case on the counter next to a small Gladstone bag of his own.

Meanwhile John Pull went to a room at the rear to put the kettle on to make the morning tea.

A 10 a.m. the cashier opened the bank for business, which he thought would be anything but brisk. The wet and windy morning had deterred all but the hardiest shoppers from turning out. The shopping centre seemed almost deserted.

So it was with surprise that the cashier looked up as two young men in raincoats walked in. He had never seen them before, and his surprise increased as they casually strolled through the gate and into the office area at the rear of the bank, where they stood looking around

"What's all this about?" the cashier said. The two young men didn't reply.

At that moment John Pull came out from the back, kettle in hand. He gasped in astonishment when he saw the older of the two youths, standing only a few feet from him.

"You're not supposed to come back here," Pull said.

The youth produced a short-barrelled shotgun from under his raincoat. As John Pull raised an arm as if to protect himself, the youth took a step back and fired. The blast struck the guard above the left eye. He dropped the kettle and slumped to the floor.

The youths then turned to the shocked cashier at the counter. "Where's the money?" the younger one demanded.

"In the case," the cashier told him, his voice quavering.

The youth went behind the counter and picked up the Gladstone bag. Then both made for the door.

"No – not that – the attaché case," the terrified young cashier stammered.

The youth came back, exchanged the Gladstone for the attaché case, and then followed his partner outside.

The cashier ran to the bank guard. John Pull lay face-down, his head in a pool of blood. The cashier ran to the front door. Through the rain he saw a small green car driving away. He rushed back into the bank and dialled 999.

"The bank has been robbed! A man has been shot!"

He hurried behind the counter again and stepped on the alarm button. As the bell began to clatter he ran next door to a shop where the proprietor was having his morning tea.

"Why are you always testing that burglar alarm?" the shopkeeper asked.

"It's not a test – the bank has been robbed!" the

cashier told him. "And the guard..."

"Are you joking?" the shopkeeper interrupted. Then, realising that this was serious, he ran to the bank with the cashier, knelt beside John Pull and lifted him in his arms. The guard's head was covered with blood, but he was moving slightly. The cashier brought some water and moistened the guard's lips. Then John Pull died.

Two police cars raced up to the bank. "It was two young men in a green MG Magnette," the cashier told the officers. "One of them had a shotgun."

As a car sped off in belated pursuit, Detective Superintendent Ronald Clapp arrived from Worthing with a police surgeon who confirmed that Pull was dead. The full shotgun charge had entered his forehead almost at point-blank range.

"The robbery took less than a minute," the cashier told Clapp. "I panicked when they shot the guard. I thought I'd be next."

"Why did you tell them they had taken the wrong bag?" Clapp asked.

"Sheer panic – that's the only reason I can give."

"Would you recognise the men if you saw them again?"

"Yes, I think so. The one with the gun was the leader. He was about 20. Tall, good-looking with brown hair, long at the back. He wore a sports jacket under his raincoat. The one who took the money was younger and not so tall. He had fair hair."

"Was anyone else in the getaway car?"

"I don't know. I couldn't see in the rain."

The cashier referred to a slip of paper that had been left him by the bank guard. It revealed that the attaché case contained £1,372 in notes of £5, £1 and 10-shilling denominations. He said that some of the money was banded. The case was stamped with the name of Lloyds Bank.

Then the manager arrived. He said that 56 of the pound notes were worn and mutilated, so he had bundled them together the previous day to be exchanged for new ones.

An alert was put out for the MG Magnette and for the two youths. Police throughout Sussex, Surrey, Hampshire and Kent set up roadblocks, stopping all traffic for questioning.

Shortly before midday a call came in from a Worthing taxi-driver who had heard about the bank murder over his cab radio. "I just picked up two young fellows at Worthing station," he said. "I supposed they'd come off a train. They asked to be taken to the seafront, and I dropped them there a few minutes ago. They looked nervous and kept whispering to each other. One of them paid me with a fiver from a thick wallet."

The driver added that the youths wore sweaters and jeans, and had no raincoats. They were not carrying an attaché case.

Clapp sent Sergeant Jack Grant and Constable Derek Randall to investigate. They cruised around and found two young men waiting at the bus terminal. The officers approached the pair, who identified themselves as Alan Hosier, 20, and Philip Tucker, 16, both from London. Tucker had £60 in his pockets, and Hosier had £120 in five-pound notes in his wallet.

"Where did you get this money?" Sergeant Grant asked them.

"Saved it," replied Hosier. "We both packed up our jobs to go on holiday in Cornwall."

"You were going on holiday in November, with no luggage, not even your coats?"

"Sure. Why not?"

"Have you heard about the bank robbery in Worthing?" Randall asked.

The youths looked startled. "Yes, we heard them talking about it at the station," Tucker said. "But we were on the train from London when it happened."

Grant and Randall took them to the police station and then called in the bank cashier to look at the suspects through a one-way glass panel.

"The younger fellow is one of the men," he said positively. "He's not the gunman – he's the one who took the money."

"How about the other man?" Grant asked.

"I don't recognise him."

"You're sure he wasn't the younger man's partner?"

"Yes, positive. I never saw him before."

The officers decided to question the youths separately. After the 16-year-old was taken into another room, Grant told him that the police believed he was one of the bank robbers who had killed the guard, and warned him that he might face a murder charge.

"Murder!" the youth echoed faintly. Then he blurted out: "But I didn't do it! I only went into the bank. I didn't have a gun, or do the shooting. I went into the bank and Vic had the gun, but I didn't expect it to go off."

"Who is Vic?" Grant asked.

"Vic Terry. He's from Chiswick in west London. The hold-up was his idea. He said there wouldn't be any trouble."

"How about your friend Hosier? What did he have to do with it?"

"He didn't even go into the bank. He just drove the car."

"Who else was in on the robbery?" Randall asked.

The youth hesitated. "Well, Vic's girl friend knew about it, but she didn't go along with us. She lives in Worthing. We used her home as a base."

"What's her name?"

"Valerie Salter," the youth replied, giving her address.

"Where are Terry and the girl now?"

"We decided to split up and meet later at the harbour in Portsmouth. Hosier and I left them at her house."

It was now 12.50 p.m. Clapp ordered a four-county alert for the couple, who might be in a green MG Magnette.

Five minutes later a taxi-driver passing the bus station at Littlehampton, 10 miles west of Worthing, was flagged down by a young man wearing a sports coat and a girl in a black cardigan. They had just alighted from a bus from Worthing. As they got into the taxi the young man said: "We want to go to Portsmouth."

The driver had no radio. He had been out since early morning and had heard nothing of the bank murder. He headed down the coast road to Portsmouth, 25 miles to the west. In his mirror he could see that the youth had his arm around the girl and that they were smiling at each other. The girl was about 18 and not particularly pretty, but she had a fresh, radiant look. He suspected that they were off for a weekend together.

Suddenly the cabbie saw a police car drawn up across the road. A uniformed officer was waving him down. He stopped. A police sergeant came up to the car and peered into the back seat. In the mirror the cabbie saw the couple were still snuggled close together, watching the sergeant silently.

"All right, drive on," the sergeant said.

"Who are you looking for?" the cabbie asked.

"Never mind. Everything's all right." There were other cars behind and the officer waved the cab on.

When they had gone a few miles the young man leaned forward and said: "We want to go to the ferry at Portsmouth, where the boats come in."

"You mean the ferry to the Isle of Wight?"

"Yes."

A few miles on the taxi stopped at another roadblock, just outside Barnham. Again, after glancing in the back seat, a police officer motioned the driver to proceed. Glancing in his mirror, the cabbie saw that the couple seemed to be completely engrossed in each other. Then, as he approached Chichester, he saw two more police cars positioned diagonally across the road. He stopped again and a sergeant opened the back door of the taxi. With him were two constables.

"What are your names?" the sergeant asked the passengers.

"James Diamond," the youth replied, giving a surname that was later to become significant. "This is my wife."

"Where are you going?"

"Portsmouth."

The sergeant glanced at the plaid bag but did not

examine it. He closed the door again. "All right, you can go on your way," he told the cabbie.

"What's the trouble?" the cabbie asked.

"A bank guard was shot and killed in Worthing, but we're looking for two men."

As the cabbie pulled away the young man in the back seat said: "So a bank guard was killed. That's too bad. I wonder who did it?"

"Whoever it was they'll probably catch him at one of these roadblocks," the cabbie said.

"Yes, I suppose they will." The youth paused and then said: "By the way, what's the train fare to Scotland?"

"I wouldn't know. I suppose about £30."

The youth fell silent again. At about 2.15 p.m. they reached the pier for the Isle of Wight ferry and the couple got out and paid their fare. Then the cabbie turned back for Littlehampton.

The officers at the roadblocks later learned that a man and girl were now being sought.

Meanwhile, at about 2 p.m. a green MG Magnette was found parked about a mile from Valerie Salter's home in Worthing. A check on the licence number revealed that the car was stolen the day before – in Chiswick, where Victor Terry lived. Inside the car were the attaché case, and a gun from which the bolt had been removed.

Valerie's mother was contacted at work and driven home by police. She told Detective Superintendent Clapp that the three youths came to the house at about 8 a.m. asking for Valerie. She gave them a cup of tea.

"She has known Victor Terry for about three months," the mother said. "She has visited him several times at his parents' home in Chiswick. Victor introduced the other boys to me this morning. Then Valerie told me to tell her boss that she wouldn't be in to work today. She said she wanted to stay at home with Victor. I went out – and that's all I know."

Searching her daughter's room, the police found the girl's wardrobe locked, and they removed the screws from the hinges. Inside were three men's raincoats, one of which contained the bolt of a gun and 14 cartridges.

They also found a handbag containing £100 in fivers.

Further questioning of the two youths in custody produced Victor Terry's address in Chiswick and the names of places that he frequented. The suspects said that Terry could be identified by four words tattooed on his right arm – Vic, Maureen, Knife and Mabel.

Clapp now believed that Terry and the girl could have eluded the police blockade and gone to west London. He asked the Metropolitan Police to search for them there, and scores of officers were sent to Chiswick. The questioning of Terry's parents and his friends brought no results, so the police went from one pub to another that evening, asking young men to show their right arms. Meanwhile, Scotland Yard's Detective Superintendent Bob Acott and Detective Sergeant Alan Rudd arrived in Worthing to lead the investigation, and the manhunt continued throughout the night.

At 10 a.m. on Friday, the morning after the murder, a young man and a girl left a boarding-house in Portsmouth, where they had spent the night. They signed the guest book as Mr. and Mrs. J. Diamond of Ealing. At breakfast they told the landlady that they were on their honeymoon. Then they went out to the street, where a taxi the young man had ordered was waiting.

"My wife and I want to go to Yeovil in Somerset," the young man told the driver. "Is that all right with you?"

The cabbie was aware that Yeovil was a good 70 miles away. "It's OK by me," he said. "As long as you can pay the fare."

"Don't worry about that."

The cabbie drove west. He had read in the newspaper about the young couple wanted for the bank murder in Worthing, but his passengers did not seem to match the descriptions. The man was wearing a lightweight overcoat and the girl a suede jacket as they sat on the back seat, holding hands and smiling at each other.

As he drove on the cabbie noticed police cars drawn up beside the road. Officers were standing beside them, watching each car that passed. But no one stopped him.

He reached Salisbury around midday and the young man suggested they stop for something to eat. They all went to a restaurant together and had lunch. At the table the youth said casually that he and his wife were on their honeymoon.

"I'm planning to do a bit of shooting," he said. "I want to buy a gun."

The cabbie drove around the town until they came to a sporting goods shop. They all went in and the young man chose a .410 shotgun and 100 cartridges. The shop assistant told him that he would need a licence. He went to a nearby post office and came back with a licence bearing the name of J. Diamond, with an address in Ealing. Having bought the gun, they all returned to the taxi and drove on towards Yeovil.

"How much would you charge to take us on a tour of Devon and Cornwall?" the youth asked suddenly.

"I'll have to call my office and find out," the cabbie said. He found a roadside phone box and called his office in Portsmouth.

"Where are you now?" his boss asked.

"Somewhere east of Yeovil."

"Well, take them wherever they want to go and phone me later. I'll see that the price is reasonable."

But when the cabbie returned to his vehicle the young man had changed his plans. He told the cabbie to head north and just drive.

They travelled north on minor roads throughout the afternoon. The cabbie became lost several times. Finally he was told to go to Oxford. When they got there his passengers told him to take the main highway east into London. When the cabbie got lost again on the western outskirts of London the youth said abruptly, "That's all right. Drop us here."

The couple got out and the youth paid the fare of £15 with three five-pound notes. It was 5.30 p.m. as the cabbie watched them disappear into a crowd. He drove around until he found himself at Marble Arch, where he phoned his boss again.

"What are you doing in west London?" his boss

demanded. "And where are your passengers?"

"I just dropped them off."

"Well, report to the police at once. You've been driving around with the Worthing bank murderer."

When the cabbie had phoned earlier about his honeymoon couple, the Worthing Police had just received a call from the Littlehampton cab driver, who said he thought he had driven Victor Terry and Valerie Salter to Portsmouth the previous afternoon. Portsmouth Police had then phoned local taxi companies and told them to have their drivers keep a lookout for the couple.

And from the touring cabbie's reports it became apparent that he had picked up the fugitives. After ordering the cabbie to "take them where they want to go," his employer notified the police that he believed the couple were in one of his taxis, number YMX 14, near Yeovil and headed for Devon and Cornwall.

Roadblocks were set up in the two counties, and throughout the afternoon hundreds of police officers searched for the taxi, which by then had changed direction, and was heading north.

Detective Superintendent Acott notified Scotland Yard of the new development. With a suspected murderer at large, presumably armed, the Yard sent armed detectives into the Chiswick and Hounslow areas. Weekend leave was cancelled for most of London's 15,000 police. All who could be spared were assigned to west London, where a house-to-house search began near Victor Terry's home.

Meanwhile the cabbie criss-crossed the area in a car with police officers, trying to find the corner where he dropped the couple. But he was lost at the time, and he couldn't find the place again.

That evening Valerie Salter's mother appeared on TV, appealing to her daughter to leave Victor Terry, give herself up, and help the police. A picture of the girl was shown and the public was asked to join in the search for her. It was also announced that Lloyds Bank were offering a reward of £10,000 for information leading to the arrest, and conviction, of John Pull's killer.

Detective Superintendent Acott ordered the manhunt to be extended to the whole of England, and by the following morning 68,000 police from Cornwall to the Scottish border were actively engaged in the search. It had become one of the most extensive manhunts in British criminal history.

At 8 o'clock that morning a taxi drove up to the Lyndock Hotel in Glasgow. "I've got a young couple in my taxi – picked them up at the railway station," the driver told the hotel's lady owner. "Have you got a room for them?"

The Lyndock was a staid hotel in a quiet back street near Glasgow University. The owner often turned away guests whose appearance she did not like. "Well, I do have a vacant room," she said. "Do they look like nice quiet people?"

The taxi-driver grinned. "They're on their honeymoon. They'll be too busy to cause you any trouble."

"Tell them to come in," the owner said. "I've got a lovely big double room they can have."

The couple were ushered to the reception desk, where the owner was somewhat perturbed to discover that their only luggage was a holdall bag. But she liked their looks and told the young man to sign the register. He signed "Mr. and Mrs. Parker," with an address in Manchester. After he paid her £6. 10s for two nights she showed them to a comfortable room on the second floor.

"We're tired from the train journey," the young man said. "We'll probably be sleeping most of the time."

"That's quite all right," the hotel owner said. "I want you to feel at home here."

She saw the honeymooners again at 3 p.m., when they said they were going to the pictures. They returned at seven o'clock and had dinner at the hotel.

"Would you like to come into my sitting-room and watch television with me this evening?" she inquired They accepted and sat on a divan together to watch *Juke Box Jury*. Then the young man began to yawn.

"We're still a little tired," he said. "I think we'll go to bed."

Shortly after they went back upstairs, the hotel owner's cousin and his wife, who were visiting, came into the room. They sat up together until quite late, watching a TV film. Then the news came on. There was a taped recording of the appeal from Valerie's mother to her daughter to leave Victor Terry and go to the police. The girl's picture was flashed on to the screen.

"Why – that's Mrs. Parker!" the owner gasped. "Then Mr. Parker must be Victor Terry – the Worthing bank killer!"

Her cousin drove her to the Marine police station where she was shown a photograph of Valerie Salter. "That's the girl," she told the police. "She's in my hotel, in room seven."

Four police officers led by Detective Inspector Hector MacDougall returned to the hotel with her at 1 a.m. None of them was armed. They went to room seven and knocked. After a moment a young man in his underwear came to the door. In the bed behind him a frightened girl was pulling the covers up to her chin.

"We're police officers," MacDougall announced. "Are you Victor Terry?"

The youth hesitated. Then he quietly answered, "Yes." The officers asked him to show them his right arm. It bore the tattoos.

The couple were told to get dressed and then the girl identified herself as Valerie Salter. Searching her red and green plaid bag, the officers found £928 in notes, some of them still banded together. And 56 of the notes were old and mutilated.

No weapon was found in the room. Terry had left the shotgun he bought in Salisbury in the Glasgow taxi.

MacDougall telephoned Detective Superintendent Acott in Worthing, who arranged for arrest warrants to be issued for the couple. Terry was charged with the murder of John Pull and the girl was charged with receiving £928, knowing it to have been stolen. The pair were flown to London late that afternoon and driven from there to Worthing. At the police station Terry made a statement in which he attempted to exonerate his girl friend.

"I want to tell you I did the job and she knew nothing about it," he said. "She did not know the money was stolen – and she never carried the bag. I carried it and she never touched it."

He then admitted shooting John Pull, but he claimed that the bank guard grabbed the barrel of the gun and attempted to push it away. He had his finger on the trigger, he said, and the gun went off accidentally.

Valerie Salter said she took no part in the actual robbery. But she was aware that it was planned – and she knew when the youths returned with the money it had been stolen from the bank. She said she knew nothing of the murder until she and Terry reached Chichester in the taxi. Then she heard a police officer tell the cabbie that a bank guard had been murdered. She claimed that when they reached Portsmouth she asked Terry about this, and he told her, "I did the shooting, but I had no intention of killing the man."

By now Alan Hosier and Philip Tucker had signed statements concerning their part in the robbery. Both had already been charged with murder and were being held in jail.

The three youths and the girl were brought before Worthing magistrates on December 7th. Victor Terry, Hosier and Tucker were now charged with armed robbery and murder, and Valerie Salter with receiving the stolen money and being an accessory after the fact of murder. Though he was only 16, Tucker was to be tried as an adult. All four pleaded not guilty.

Identifying Terry and Tucker as the men who entered the bank, the cashier testified that the guard did not seize the barrel of the gun or make any attempt to struggle with Terry during the hold-up. His evidence was supported by the findings of the Metropolitan Police laboratory. The only fingerprints found on the gun were those of Victor Terry.

The prosecutor produced a palm-print of Terry's,

found on the door of the bank, and fingerprints of the other two youths found in the stolen car.

The bank manager identified the £56 in old and mutilated currency found in the girl's plaid bag as notes he had banded together on the afternoon before the robbery. All four defendants were remanded in custody.

When they appeared in the dock at Lewes Assizes on March 20th, 1961, Terry was charged with capital murder in the furtherance of theft; Tucker and Hosier with murder; and Valerie Salter with harbouring and assisting Terry, knowing that he shot and killed the bank guard.

Asked to explain why he called the robbers back to collect the attaché case instead of the Gladstone bag, the cashier told the court: "The thought occurred to me that should the man discover the mistake the consequences might not have been too pleasant."

"You wanted to get rid of him at all costs," observed Mr. Justice Stable. "I am not surprised."

Mr. Geoffrey Lawrence, prosecuting, said Terry entered the bank with a loaded gun and both Hosier and Tucker knew he possessed it, and that it was loaded, and that if necessary he would use it. After the bank raiders had split the proceeds of the robbery, Tucker and Hosier had become unstuck through being too generous. The suspicions of the taxi-driver who tipped off the police were aroused when they gave him a 10-shilling note for a half-crown fare and told him to keep the change.

Terry and Valerie Salter saw the pair being questioned by police on Worthing seafront, so after stopping off at the girl's home they caught a bus to Littlehampton.

Entering a plea of not guilty by reason of insanity on behalf of Terry, Mr. Alan King-Hamilton QC, defending, said his client believed himself to be possessed by the spirit of "Legs" Diamond, the notorious American gangster of the 1930s. Terry was a drug addict, said his counsel, who suffered from hallucinations, displayed symptoms of schizophrenia, and had held a grudge

Demonstrations outside Pentonville Prison against the hanging of Ronald Marwood. The killer (left) complained about the noise in the prison

Harry, after retirement, outside Strangeways Prison, Manchester

Harry and Doris on their wedding day

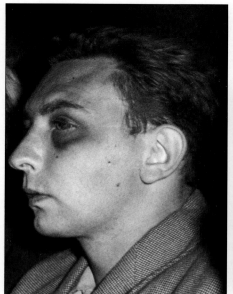

Above, police killer Guenther Podola and his arrest at a London hotel. Below, outside Wandsworth Prison on the morning of his hanging

Harry and Doris being wined and dined at the Imperial Hotel in Blackpool. Their hosts were German newspaper reporters interested in Harry's story. Right, Harry in a pub of friend Joe Rix

Shrewsbury Prison at the time of the hanging of George Riley (inset)

Russell Pascoe

Dennis Whitty

Harry and Doris at a charity function on July 29th, 1964. Two weeks later Harry would carry out his last execution at Strangeways

The contents of Harry's briefcase; pliers, ruler, diary and tape. Also shown are bow-ties Harry would wear

Michael Gregsten's body in a lay-by beside the A6. Above, Peter Alphon and right, James Hanratty – the first suspects in the murder

Harry and Doris enjoying their retirement

Peter Allen (left) and Gwynne Evans – the last men to hang

against the world ever since he was a child. This stemmed from his dogs being taken away and destroyed for attacking children. The incident gave him a persecution complex.

He was a criminal by the age of eight, leading a gang of children. His first conviction followed when he was 10, and at 18 he was sent to borstal for bludgeoning an elderly man with a sand-filled sock and robbing him of £10.

When he registered under the name of Diamond at a Portsmouth boarding-house, "it was not Victor Terry and his girl friend, but Legs Diamond and his moll," said Mr. King-Hamilton.

A psychiatrist called by the defence said that Terry was suffering from diminished responsibility when he committed the murder, but he knew what he was doing, that it was wrong, and in law he was therefore not insane. Medical experts testifying for the prosecution said that Terry was sane, showing no symptoms of any disease of the mind that would deprive him of responsibility.

Tucker and Hosier both told the court that Terry assured them the gun would not be loaded. Tucker said that as they drove to the bank Terry had sat fiddling with the weapon, saying repeatedly: "I'm the fastest man in Texas."

"Tell me," the judge asked Tucker, "what do you think a bank guard should do when two young man go into a bank holding a gun?"

"He should not have done anything," Tucker replied. "He was being held up."

"Are you now blaming Mr. Pull for his death?"

"Yes."

"It's all his own fault?"

"No, you cannot say it was all his own fault, for if we had not gone in he would not have been dead."

In tears, Valerie Salter told the court that she knew Terry was a drug-user, and hoped that her influence might settle him down. She admitted she was told about the bank robbery in advance. Terry said they would make a lot of money, buy a house and marry right away.

When Mr. Lawrence asked her why she had not gone to the police, her reply took his breath away. "I don't believe it is a criminal offence to rob a bank," she said.

Hardly able to believe his ears, the prosecutor asked her to repeat this.

Asked why she continued to accompany Terry when she knew the outcome of the robbery, she said in a whisper: "I did not want to go, but I could not help myself."

"You were so infatuated you would have gone anywhere with him?" asked the judge.

"Yes, I am afraid so."

In his concluding speech for Terry, Mr. King-Hamilton sought a verdict of manslaughter by reason of diminished responsibility. "If other people think they are the Duke of Wellington or Napoleon Bonaparte and say they hear voices, what is so odd about Terry hearing the voice of Legs Diamond?" he asked.

For the prosecution, Mr. Lawrence described Terry as ruthless, callous, cunning and the raid's mastermind. "At all stages he was in control. The raid may not have been conceived with the tactical brilliance of, say, Field Marshal Montgomery, but it was carefully planned over a long period."

Mr. Justice Stable reminded the jury that they were not refereeing a football match or listening to a detective story. They were dealing with reality in which lives were at stake.

After retiring for two and a half hours the jury returned to find Victor Terry guilty of capital murder, and he was sentenced to death. Hosier and Tucker were convicted of murder, for which Hosier was sentenced to life imprisonment and Tucker was ordered to be detained during Her Majesty's pleasure.

Found guilty of being an accessory, Valerie Salter was placed on probation for a year. "Go back to your family and friends and start life afresh," the judge told her.

The authorities were unaware that the murder of John

Pull was a chilling echo of an unrelated killing by Victor Terry's friend Francis "Flossie" Forsyth, an 18-year-old road worker. Some five months before the Worthing bank raid Forsyth was one of four young men who robbed and killed 23-year-old Alan Jee in Hounslow, Middlesex.

After a drinking session at the Clay Pigeon Inn at Eastcote, near Uxbridge, they waylaid Mr. Jee in an alley. Forsyth later told a teenage friend what had happened, the youth informed the police, and the four were arrested and charged with murder.

One of them, Norman Harris, an unemployed driver aged 23, told the police: "I'm the oldest, so it's bound to be down to me. If it all comes out, I think I'll dangle. I will not tell you who put the boot in. All I did was hold him and go through his pockets."

"It was me that did the kicking," Forsyth admitted. "I didn't think I'd hurt him that much. I only kicked him twice to keep him quiet. These are the shoes I had on that night. Look, they're only soft ones."

But the victim's skull had been fractured, and he died next day of a cerebral contusion.

All four young men denied capital murder when they were brought to trial at the Old Bailey on September 20th, 1960. Forsyth expected no more than a five-year jail sentence. Only Harris feared the worst, and his fears were confirmed when he and Forsyth were convicted of capital murder in the furtherance of theft, and sentenced to death.

Christopher Darby, a 20-year-old coalman, was sentenced to life imprisonment for non-capital murder, and 17-year-old Terence Lutt, an unemployed labourer, was convicted of capital murder and, too young to be hanged, was ordered to be detained during Her Majesty's pleasure.

Forsyth was hanged by Harry Allen at Wandsworth, with Samuel Plant assisting, and Harris was hanged at Pentonville by Robert Stewart, with Harry Robinson as his assistant. Forsyth's pal Victor Terry was clearly aware of this when, less than two hours later, he produced his revolver from under his raincoat and murdered bank guard John Pull.

Six months after that, at 8 a.m. on May 25th, 1961, Harry executed Victor Terry at Wandsworth.

The chief executioner escorted five more condemned men to the scaffold before that year was out. A month after Victor Terry, on June 29th, Harry despatched Zsiga Pankotai at Leeds Prison. A week later, on July 6th, he executed Edwin Bush, who murdered Elsie Batten in her Charing Cross Road, London, antiques shop. Bush, hanged at Pentonville, was the first person convicted of murder after being identified by an Identikit portrait.

Harry flew from Manchester to Belfast that same month to hang Samuel McLaughlin at Belfast Prison on July 25th. McLaughlin was found guilty of murdering his wife Nellie. After that, Harry performed the last execution to take place in London when he hanged Hendryk Niemasz at Wandsworth Prison on September 8th. Niemasz was convicted of murdering Alice Buxton and her husband Hubert.

For Harry's last execution – the eighth – of that year, he again flew to Belfast, this time to execute Robert McGladdery on December 4th. McGladdery had pleaded not guilty to the murder of 19-year-old Pearl Gamble, but made a full confession the day before he was executed.

CHAPTER 8

TRAGEDY AT DEADMAN'S HILL

Few episodes in the history of crime in the 20th century aroused so much controversy as the trial and execution of the A6 murderer James Hanratty. The case that traversed almost 40 years, from 1961 until 1999, inspired books, TV programmes, magazine articles, protests and counter-protests, and finally produced a clear-cut result that showed the police and law-enforcement authorities had got it absolutely right.

Others, however, including some distinguished writers and journalists, had got it all wrong. Their vociferous campaign that the wrong man was hanged revealed the exact opposite – the right man was hanged.

The controversy was reaching its zenith when on April 3rd, 1962, Harry Allen arrived at Bedford Prison. Next day he was due to hang Hanratty, the man whom a jury had found guilty of killing an innocent man and maiming his lover for life.

"You've got it all wrong," chanted the pro-Hanratty brigade. And they never stopped. Thirty-six years later, the *Daily Mirror* headline in November, 1997, proclaimed: "Hanratty to be cleared after 36 years."

That would be nearly four decades too late to save James Hanratty's neck, for Harry Allen had long since despatched the 25-year-old small-time crook.

Ever since his trial Hanratty's family and various supporters had expressed doubts about his guilt. The campaign was orchestrated over the years by celebrities such as investigative reporter Paul Foot, lawyers including Leon Blom-Cooper, and even John Lennon from the Beatles. With its many twists and turns, the case became one of the most bizarre in British criminal history, and there would be more surprises 40 years after the shooting.

The lovers at the centre of the tragedy were colleagues

– Michael Gregsten, a 34-year-old scientist at the Road Research laboratory near Slough, and Valerie Storie, 22, a research assistant at the same laboratory.

Michael Gregsten was married with two children. His wife Janet knew about his affair and was later to claim indifference, saying she simply regarded Valerie as her husband's "bit on the side."

Gregsten's car was a grey Morris Minor that he had borrowed from an aunt. On the evening of Tuesday, August 22nd, 1961, he drove Valerie to a pub they often visited, the Old Station Inn at Taplow, Buckinghamshire. Leaving at about 9.20, they drove to a cornfield near Taplow, another trysting place they often used.

They had been there for about 30 minutes when a man rapped on the car's side window. He was smartly dressed, with a handkerchief obscuring the lower half of his face.

When Gregsten wound down the driver's window, the man thrust in a gun and said, "This is a hold-up. I am a desperate man." He added that he had been on the run for four months, and if the couple did as they were told they would be all right. He got into the rear, holding the revolver to Gregsten's back. What happened over the next few hours was a living nightmare.

The man said he was hungry and had not eaten for two days, and that his revolver was a .38. The couple offered to drive him to where he could eat, but he said, "It's all right, there is no hurry."

Valerie noticed that he kept looking at his watch. After about five minutes he told Gregsten to drive further into the cornfield. He then ordered then both to hand over their money and watches, pocketing £3 from Gregsten's wallet. But Valerie managed to take £7 from her shopping basket, hiding the notes in her bra.

Over the next two hours the man talked in brief bursts. "Jim," as he said his name was, told Gregsten and Valerie that he had been to remand homes and borstal and had done five years' CT (corrective training) and expected to get PD (preventive detention) next.

He told Gregsten to get into the car's boot, but Valerie

protested, saying the exhaust was defective and he could be asphyxiated. Changing his mind, the gunman ordered Gregsten to drive towards Slough. They arrived there at 11.45 p.m. and stopped briefly at a milk machine, but they lacked the necessary coins.

The gunman ordered Gregsten to drive on, through Hayes and Greenford, heading towards London. Near London Airport they pulled into a garage for petrol. In Stanmore, Gregsten was allowed to leave the car to get cigarettes from a machine. He did not take the opportunity to run away or call for help because Valerie was being held hostage.

The nightmare journey continued, some 30 miles in all, through St. Albans, along the A6 to Luton and Bedford. At one point Gregsten flashed his reversing light to attract attention. Another car drew alongside, its passenger pointing to the back of the Morris Minor. Gregsten stopped and got out with the gunman to check the rear lights.

Valerie could have slipped behind the wheel and driven off. She didn't, she was later to say, because she couldn't bring herself to abandon Gregsten.

The gunman said he wanted a "kip," and when they came to a lay-by at Deadman's Hill, Bedfordshire, he ordered Gregsten to park. He discussed tying the couple up while he slept and they begged him not to shoot them.

"If I was going to shoot you I would have done it before now," he told them. He bundled Gregsten out of the car to search the boot for rope. Failing to find any, he tied Valerie's wrists together with her lover's tie. When he told Gregsten to pass a duffel bag to the rear seat of the car, Gregsten leaned to pick it up, then turned, perhaps intending to hurl it at the gunman. "Jim" fired two shots into his head, killing him instantly. The time was 3 a.m.

Valerie screamed, "You shot him, you bastard! Why did you do that?"

"He frightened me. He moved too quick!"

Valerie begged the man to get a doctor, but he

snapped, "Be quiet, will you! I'm finking."

In earlier conversations Valerie had noticed that Jim habitually pronounced "f" for "th." There followed an hysterical conversation about whether or not Gregsten was dead, and then the gunman ordered Valerie to kiss him. At that moment she saw his full face for the first time in the headlights of a passing car.

He forced Valerie to join him in the back seat, where he raped her. Then he made her help him drag Gregsten's body out of the car. They laid the body on the concrete close to the verge, and Valerie sat beside it, pleading for the man to leave her alone.

"There is no hurry," he said coolly, and asked her to start the car and show him how the gears worked. Then he fired a volley of shots at her from a range of six feet. She fell and heard a clicking sound as he reloaded his revolver. More shots were fired, all of which went over her head. He approached her and kicked her lightly, but Valerie lay still, feigning death.

The man then got into the car and drove off towards Luton.

It was now about four in the morning and Valerie Storie discovered that she was paralysed, unable to move her arms and legs. She lay there for hours, hoping that a passing motorist would stop, but eventually lost consciousness.

She was discovered at 6.45 a.m. by a farm labourer walking along the A6 on his way to work. He alerted a student doing a traffic census farther down the road, and the student flagged down a motorist who went to a phone box and dialled 999.

The student knelt at Valerie's side as she gasped out a few details of her ordeal. He jotted down what she said on the back of one of his enumerator forms and handed it to a senior police officer at 8 a.m. It was the first description of the killer: "Fairish brown hair and staring eyes."

By 7 a.m. the police, led by Inspector Edward Milborrow, had arrived on the scene and Valerie told him what had happened. An alert was flashed to all police forces to be on the lookout for the Morris Minor.

Valerie Storie was admitted to Bedford Hospital at 7.45 a.m. The consultant surgeon found her to be remarkably lucid and able to talk clearly about her ordeal, despite having bullets in her body and being paralysed. He allowed senior police officers to take a statement from her.

The bullets that had struck her had caused massive damage but had also had the effect of anaesthetising her to the pain and shock of her injury. She gave Detective Inspector Whiffen a description of the man who had killed her lover and raped her.

The description was never made public and the inspector was not asked about it at the trial. However, as a result of what Valerie said, the press and public were alerted to look for a man aged 25, 5ft 6in, of medium build, with a pale face, deep-set brown eyes and an East End accent.

At 3 p.m. Detective Superintendent Bob Acott of Scotland Yard's Murder Squad arrived at Deadman's Hill to take charge of the inquiry, and at 6.30 that evening the missing Morris Minor was found abandoned at Redbridge. On its floor were two cartridge cases, and two large clots of blood.

Witnesses were traced who had seen the car being driven to where it was dumped. From their descriptions of the driver, an Identikit picture was issued. The witnesses said they had seen him at 7 a.m., which was an important clue. Deadman's Hill is 50 miles from Redbridge, and a poor driver, at night, would have taken three hours to do the journey by side roads. This suggested that the man seen driving the car was the killer.

The following morning a cleaner found a fully loaded revolver and five boxes of ammunition under a 36A bus seat in a London Transport garage in Peckham. Ballistics proved it was the weapon used to murder Michael Gregsten.

The route of the 36A bus was a clue in itself. It

travelled between Peckham, Kilburn, Marble Arch and Paddington Station, passing within 100 yards of the Vienna Hotel in Maida Vale. This establishment would crop up again and again during the investigation. Somewhere along that route the killer boarded the bus and dumped the gun.

By Saturday morning, August 26th, Superintendent Acott was interviewing Valerie Storie. He called a police expert to her bedside to construct an Identikit picture from her description of the killer. He also publicly appealed to landlords and landladies, asking them, "Do you have a lodger who has not gone out for the last few days?" At that precise moment, a woman staying at the Alexandria Court Hotel in Seven Sisters Road, Finsbury Park, complained to the manager about the behaviour of the man in the room next to hers. This man kept her awake at night by walking about and talking to himself. He had booked in on August 23rd, the evening of the day of the murder.

A routine police patrol interviewed the man, who gave his name as Frederick Durrant. His real name, however, was Peter Louis Alphon. His father was a records clerk at Scotland Yard's Aliens Department and, he said, he had booked into the Vienna Hotel in Maida Vale on the night of August 22nd after visiting his mother in Streatham. Apparently, Alphon led a nomadic existence, moving from hotel to hotel. The register at the Vienna confirmed that a man called Durrant had booked in on the 22nd, and Alphon's statement was routinely filed.

Detective Sergeant Jock Mackie, the officer detailed to draw up the Identikit picture with Valerie Storie, found it a difficult task because her description did not match that given by other witnesses. Unable to agree a single portrait, the police issued two Identikit pictures: one selected by Valerie, the second from other witnesses.

The two pictures, which differed sharply, appeared on TV and in the press on August 30th. They had one feature in common – the man's "dark, staring eyes." Every newspaper described them as brown.

On Thursday morning, August 31st, a man left his

lodgings in Boundary Road, Swiss Cottage, to walk to a dry-cleaners in the arcade of Swiss Cottage tube station.

Opposite the dry-cleaners was an antiques shop owned by William Ewer, brother-in-law of Janet Gregsten, who was helping him in the shop when she saw the man go into the dry-cleaners. Suddenly she pointed and said: "That's the man the police are looking for! That's the man! He fits the description."

That man was James Hanratty.

Both William Ewer and Janet Gregsten would later dismiss reports of the identification in the arcade as nonsense, but those who have researched the case in depth are convinced that the story has a basis of truth. The account of what happened came from Ewer himself.

The story was broken by Peter Duffy, a crime reporter on the *Daily Sketch*, who covered the whole case and who could not, under the rules governing contempt of court, publish the account until after the jury at Hanratty's trial had delivered their verdict. The story therefore appeared in the *Daily Sketch* on February 19th, two days after the trial ended.

Duffy reported: "The amazing intuition of Janet Gregsten, widow of A6 murder victim Michael Gregsten, helped to put James Hanratty on trial for his life. This intuition, and two fantastic coincidences which set detectives on Hanratty's trail, were revealed last night – 24 hours after he was found guilty of the A6 murder.

"Only eight days after the murder – when Scotland Yard were without a positive clue to the killer – Mrs. Gregsten pointed to Hanratty and said: 'That's the man the police are looking for.'

"Mrs. Gregsten's 50-year-old brother-in-law, William Ewer, had taken her to his antique shop [sic] in the station arcade at Swiss Cottage, north London, to try to help her get over the tragedy which had struck her life. Mrs. Gregsten had been shown an Identikit picture of a man the police wanted to interview in connection with her husband's killing.

"Her brother-in-law's shop was 21 miles from the cornfield where the A6 murder nightmare began. It was 50 miles from Deadman's Hill where the horror climaxed. Far enough away, anyone would think, to dull the memory of tragedy.

"On the morning of August 31st, Mrs. Gregsten was standing in the shop window helping Mr. Ewer hang a picture. Suddenly she clutched at Mr. Ewer's arm and pointed through the window to a man with jet black hair walking into a cleaner's shop only two yards across the arcade. 'That's the man. He fits the description,' she said. 'But it's more than that. I've got an overpowering feeling that it's him.'

"Said Mr. Ewer last night, 'I calmed her down and told her she was overwrought. But she was so convinced about what she had seen that I went into the cleaners later and talked to the manageress. She told me that the man had brought a green suit in on August 21st to have a tear in the coat mended and the trousers tapered. He had called in that day to ask if it was ready. He gave the name J. Ryan, and an address in St. John's Wood.

"Neither Mr. Ewer nor the police knew that J. Ryan was an alias of James Hanratty and that immediately after the murder he stayed, in the road named, with his friend Charles France – only a mile away from the cleaners.

"Said Mr. Ewer: 'So convinced was I about what Janet had seen that I vowed then to watch for the man myself. I had to find him again!'"

In his study of the case, *Who Killed Hanratty?*, Paul Foot recalls:

"Mr. Ewer's hunt, according to the story, did not last long. The next day he went to a café in the Finchley Road. As he sat drinking a cup of tea and pondering the almost hopelessness of the A6 murder he spotted a pair of hand-made Italian shoes. Then he found himself staring into those blue eyes again. It was the same man.

"Stunned by this miracle, according to the story, Mr. Ewer decided to follow the man. He watched him go into a florist's shop in the Finchley Road. Then, acting on an impulse, he rang Scotland Yard. The police came and made inquiries at the florist's shop, and the manageress told them that the man had come in on September 1st wanting to send some roses to his mother – a Mrs. Hanratty of 12 Sycamore Grove, Kingsbury."

The *Sketch*'s story continued: "A report was made to Scotland Yard. But the Murder Squad had never heard of Jimmy Ryan. They had never heard of the address in Sycamore Grove, Kingsbury, which was the home of his mother. But Bill Ewer could not rest. Almost daily he went out looking for the man with the staring eyes.

"He walked into the shop of a business associate in Greek Street, Soho. He did not know that Hanratty, who the Greek Street dealer had befriended, had been in the shop only that morning."

The publication of this story was the first indication that Scotland Yard had Hanratty's name and his alias long before they started to hunt him as the murderer. The only description of the killer had been released on the day of the murder, and did not fit Hanratty. Neither of the Identikit pictures resembled him. Yet here was Mrs. Gregsten "identifying" James Hanratty as he walked into the cleaners opposite her brother-in-law's shop.

The coincidence is compounded when Hanratty appears the next day in the same café as Mr. Ewer and goes into a florist's shop, giving the address of his parents.

So what enabled Mrs. Gregsten to recognise Hanratty as her husband's killer and put her brother-in-law on his trail? The *Daily Mail* reported: "The face in the crowd that caught the eye of Janet Gregsten left her gasping.

"Was it, could it be, the face of the man who only eight days before had cold-bloodedly murdered her husband? She saw the blue staring eyes when she suddenly looked out of the window…It was a flash of intuitive recognition."

Both William Ewer and Janet Gregsten attempted to rubbish the story as an invention of the popular press.

But as Bob Woffinden says in his book *Hanratty: The Final Verdict:* "If one thing is certain about this curious episode, it is that the press did not invent it. Years later, I tried to establish precisely what had occurred. It did not originally concern the *Sketch* journalist Peter Duffy.

"Early one evening, in the last week of the trial, George Hollingbery of the *Evening News* and Bernard Jordan, of the *Daily Mail*, were having a drink in the King's Head pub. Unusually, there were no other reporters present. William Ewer walked in and buttonholed them. 'We'd noticed this man before,' said Hollingbery. 'He was always fussing and taking a keen interest in the trial the whole time. 'He was always there, and so that evening when he came in the pub we knew who he was but this was the first time we had spoken to him.'

"Jordan bought him a drink, and Ewer then regaled them with this tale. This came completely out of the blue. It was something quite new and dramatic. 'None of us made a move, to make notes of anything, because we thought it might frighten him off. We just let him speak.'

"When Ewer went, the two journalists wrote down what he had said and agreed to keep it to themselves. But, according to Woffinden, Jordan did not keep his part of the pledge. He and Peter Duffy were very good friends...Jordan felt he couldn't leave him out in the cold. So he let him in on the story."

Almost five years later Duffy was asked by John Morgan on BBC1's *Panorama:* "Doesn't it seem an extraordinary coincidence that Mrs. Gregsten, having only the Identikit to go on, which doesn't look very much like James Hanratty, should look out and discover a man who is eventually convicted as her husband's murderer?"

Duffy replied: "It's something that is completely inexplicable."

In his book Woffinden points out that there was no suggestion that it may have been an error. But the whole question of identification had its problems.

Until August 31st Valerie Storie had consistently told the police that the killer had deep-set brown eyes. On August 31st she was transferred to Guy's Hospital, London. While she was in the ambulance, Bedfordshire Police issued a new description of the killer. The man now had large, icy-blue, saucer-like eyes.

This has been described as "a dramatic change," but was it really? What sort of memory retention does a woman have about her attacker when she is being raped on the back seat of a car in almost complete darkness after watching her lover shot dead in cold blood? The salient point about Hanratty was always remembered by Valerie – he had deep, staring eyes. If they were blue, they might well have become brown in her appalling situation.

On Monday, September 11th, the manager of the Vienna Hotel, Maida Vale, sacked one of his staff after discovering money was missing from the till. He subsequently decided to inspect all the bedrooms. In Room 24 he found two .38 cartridges on an armchair. He called the police, and a ballistics check revealed that the cartridges were fired from the murder weapon. Detective Superintendent Acott went to the hotel with his team; it was to become the focal point of his inquiry.

It was discovered that on the night before the murder, Room 24 was occupied by a J. Ryan, who gave a Kingsbury address. On the night of the murder the room was occupied by Frederick Durrant – Peter Alphon. The cartridge cases had rested on that chair for 19 days because the room had apparently remained unoccupied from August 23rd until September 13th.

Acott decided to treat both men as prime suspects. His first choice was Peter Alphon. Alphon's mother was interviewed, and she said she hadn't seen her son at all on the night of the murder, which destroyed his alibi.

The sacked hotel employee gave his name as William Nudds, but that was only one of his eight known aliases. He had a long criminal record, was a notorious informer and known to be a pathological liar. Not long after Hanratty's trial he was jailed for six years.

He made several contradictory statements to Acott. In the first, on September 15th, he attempted to implicate Ryan by saying that he had seemed "in a hurry" and had asked for directions to get a 36A bus. Nudds further said he thought Durrant had occupied Room 6, but he couldn't be sure. He was telling the police what he imagined they wanted to hear.

Despite this, the police now concentrated on Alphon, even taking away for analysis a pillowcase on which his head had rested.

On September 21st the sacked hotel worker was taken to Scotland Yard for questioning. His second statement said that Durrant (Alphon) had initially occupied Room 24, a basement room, but he had requested an upstairs room, and it was arranged that he could transfer if such a room became available.

Durrant left the hotel after booking in at 1 p.m., leaving his suitcase in Room 24 and saying he wouldn't be back until late that night. He hadn't returned by 2 a.m. when Nudds went to bed, leaving a note on the reception desk telling the guest that Room 6 was now vacant.

At 9.50 a.m. Nudds went to Room 6 to see if Durrant wanted breakfast. Durrant was getting dressed. Nudds asked him, "What time did you come in last night?" and Durrant replied, "Eleven o'clock," which Nudds knew to be untrue.

Nudds thought that Durrant appeared to be upset. "Ryan was at all times cool, calm and composed, whereas Durrant was hurried and agitated," he said.

On September 22nd Acott interviewed Alphon's father, telling him that officers were looking for his son. At this point the police felt sure that Alphon was the killer, because he had a history of odd behaviour, was familiar with the Slough area, and also fitted Valerie's original description.

Acott went to see Valerie Storie in hospital to keep her abreast of developments and she now told him that the killer had "icy-blue" eyes. At the magistrates' hearing

Acott played down this new description by saying: "The man having icy-blue eyes was only part of the description. It is not one we would depend on."

Why wouldn't he depend upon it? The irresistible inference was because Alphon had hazel-brown eyes. At the Hanratty trial, by which time Acott had eliminated Alphon from the inquiry, he was asked why he wanted so much to interview the missing Alphon. Acott replied: "Because we were left with two very strong suspects – Alphon and Ryan. One had to be eliminated. The only one we could eliminate was Alphon. I did not think that Alphon had done it."

So why didn't he choose to eliminate Ryan first?

Because, he said, at that point the police had not realised that J. Ryan and Hanratty were the same person.

Peter Alphon gave himself up at Scotland Yard at midnight on September 22nd. He later claimed that his interrogation lasted seven hours without rest. The police said it lasted three and a quarter hours. He was put on a number of identity parades. He was not picked out on the first, and on the second parade, Valerie Storie picked out an entirely different man.

She was questioned about this at the trial. "When it appeared that you had identified some other person on that parade, did you not afterwards say there was a fair resemblance between Alphon and the man who attacked you?"

"Some time afterwards, yes."

"Can you tell us to whom you made this observation?"

"I believe it was a doctor. I'm not sure whether it was Superintendent Acott or not."

After Alphon's interrogation, he was released without charge. Had Valerie Storie picked him out, he might well have been hanged.

On September 25th the police finally linked Ryan to James Hanratty. Charles France, Hanratty's friend, went to Scotland Yard with a postcard Hanratty had sent him from Ireland. It was France who would prove to be Hanratty's nemesis. From that day on the police kept watch on France's home and tapped his phone.

During the course of this, Acott visited Hanratty's parents at Sycamore Grove, Kingsbury, inquiring about any friends their son might have in Ireland.

The police remembered that the killer had told Valerie that he had "done the lot," which they took to mean he had served all his sentence without remission. Records revealed that only five men in the entire country had recently completed sentences without remission. One of them was James Hanratty.

Acott flew to Dublin and discovered that Hanratty had stayed in Cork and Limerick using the Ryan alias, before returning to London.

The newspapers, meanwhile, were puzzling over the switch from Alphon to Hanratty. On October 4th the *Daily Mirror* speculated: "Alphon matches almost perfectly the Identikit picture. Last night one of the theories being considered by detectives was the A6 killer spotted Alphon and tried to frame him."

This was nonsense. For the killer to have set out from the very start to frame Alphon by staying at the same hotel and planting cartridge cases there was too bizarre.

The cartridge cases – presumably left by Hanratty the day before the murder – had been fired. The prosecution suggested that Hanratty might have put in some target practice in the hotel – without waking his fellow-guests!

The prosecution wanted it both ways. Michael Gregsten's car revealed no forensic clues – no fingerprints, no fibres, nothing to link Hanratty to the car – because Hanratty had been very careful, the prosecution claimed. But if he had been so careful, why had he left clues on the bus and at the hotel? Why did he place the gun where he knew it would be found, instead of throwing it into the Thames? Why leave two cartridge cases in the hotel before the murder?

Hanratty travelled to Ireland on September 4th to get a driving licence, and he returned to London a week later. He received a lot of money from a fence, from the proceeds of robberies in Wembley and Edgware.

On September 19th he bought a car, taking the France family on trips. He was still wearing the same dark chalk-stripe suit he wore on the night of the murder. On September 30th he broke into houses in Stanmore and stole a dark jacket, disposing of his old one and wearing the stolen one over his waistcoat and trousers. He sold a diamond ring he had stolen during this period, so he was quite well off.

Then on Thursday, October 5th, he went to his usual haunt, the Rehearsal Club, where Charles France worked. There he learned he was wanted for the A6 murder. He phoned France in panic, and his friend told him to give himself up, and also tried to keep him talking so the police could trace the call.

At noon the next day Hanratty rang Superintendent Acott and said he had nothing to do with the murder. However, he refused to give himself up because he was wanted for housebreaking and had no desire to go back to prison.

He then rang the *Daily Mirror* and said substantially the same thing, adding that he was in Liverpool at the time of the murder and had three friends who could substantiate his alibi. He wouldn't name them, though, because the police also wanted them.

That evening he stole a car and drove to Liverpool, ringing Acott from a call-box when he arrived. He said he was seeking friends about his alibi. The three men, all known fences, didn't want to be implicated, he said, and he still refused to name them.

On Friday, October 6th, Acott interviewed France and his wife. France said that "Jim Ryan" had once told him that a good place to hide things was beneath the back seat of a bus.

At this point all that incriminated Hanratty in the A6 murder were the cartridge cases in the Vienna Hotel, and the fact that the killer called himself Jim and said he had done five years' CT. Hanratty had in fact done three years, and he could not have been due for "PD next" because he was too young.

The blood group of the killer – determined from semen samples – was group O. Both Hanratty and Alphon belonged to this group, which is found in 36 per cent of the population.

For the next few days Hanratty laid low. He had his hair bleached and sent flowers to his mother. Then he went to Blackpool, where he was arrested in a café by two observant constables.

Acott hurried to Blackpool. The notes taken at the interview were neither read nor signed by Hanratty, and he later denied that they were correct.

On October 13th he was put on an identity parade for the witnesses who had seen the driver of the Morris Minor. Of the four witnesses, two picked out Hanratty. They had not been present at Alphon's identity parade. The following day another identity parade was held at the foot of Valerie's hospital bed.

She spent 10 minutes examining the men closely, and then asked each to say, "Be quiet, will you! I'm finking." She picked out James Hanratty, and later that day he was charged with the murder of Michael Gregsten.

When his trial began at Bedford Assizes on January 22nd, 1962, the case against him was based almost solely on identification, and the most important witness was Valerie Storie. As she would later tell millions of TV viewers: "I was there. I was on Deadman's Hill. I know it was Hanratty."

She identified him in three ways – by sight, sound, and the description he had given of his life. She glimpsed the killer's face only once, in the glare of a car's headlights. At all other times he kept a handkerchief over his face. She told the court: "He told us to face front, presumably so that we wouldn't be able to see his face, and every time we went to turn he told us to face the front."

She was asked: "When he got out of the car and went round to the boot with Mike, were you able to see his face at all?"

"I could not see his face because he had a handkerchief or something tied irregular-fashion over his nose and mouth, presumably to stop Mike seeing him. While I was facing him, after he'd shot Mike and I was still in the car, another car came up from behind and lit up his face. He seemed to be staring through me. Very large icy-blue eyes. This was the only real proper glimpse I had of him."

She told the student who raised the alarm when she was found that the killer had "fairish brown hair." The student remembered that particularly because he asked, "Do you mean like mine?" and she replied, "Yes."

But the notes he made and gave to the police had been unaccountably lost.

The original suspect, Alphon, had fairish hair. At the time of the murder Hanratty's hair was jet black. Mrs. France had dyed it for him on August 5th, 18 days before the murder.

How accurate was Valerie Storie's memory? She told the court: "I described his eyes as icy-blue, very large. They appeared huge to me because they were just staring. Just very large, icy-blue. I could see almost the whole of the coloured part of the eye. They did not appear to be sunken back. They looked very cold blue."

Yet in early descriptions of the killer, she emphasised the man's deep-set brown eyes. Despite all this, Superintendent Acott told the jury: "Her description of the murderer has never changed from the day of the murder until now, and I have always regarded it as most reliable."

At the first identity parade at Guy's Hospital, Valerie picked out the wrong man, a man with dark, short-cropped hair. Afterwards she was heard to cry out, "I have made a mistake!"

At the trial Mr. Michael Sherrard, defending, asked her, "On the first parade you surveyed the men paraded before you for as long as five minutes before saying or doing something?"

"Yes," she replied.

"And you then identified a man as being the assassin?"

"Yes."

"Can you tell us what the man looked like?"

"No."

Yet this was a man she had seen recently, in a good light, for five minutes.

It was suggested that Hanratty, who was asked to say, "Be quiet, will you! I'm finking," was the only man on the parade who spoke with a cockney accent.

There was also Valerie's identification of the killer by what he said about himself in the car.

She told the court: "He said he'd never had a chance in life. He said that when he was a child he was locked in a cellar for days on end with only bread and water to drink. He said that since he was eight he had done remand homes, borstal, he had done CT and he next thing he would get was PD. He said, 'I have done the lot.' I believe he said he had done five years for housebreaking."

Some of this did fit Hanratty – as it would fit a great many criminals – but some of it did not. Hanratty had done CT, but he had never been to a remand home or borstal. There had never been a cellar in any house he had occupied. He first got into trouble at 16, not eight. He had done three years for housebreaking, not five.

Furthermore, Valerie declared that the man told her he could drive all sorts of cars, yet he had to ask her how to operate the gears on a Morris Minor, and he later drove badly enough to attract attention. In contrast, Hanratty was a car thief and an accomplished driver.

The murderer said he had not eaten for two days – Hanratty had breakfasted at the Vienna Hotel that morning. The man said he had been sleeping rough – Hanratty was staying at the hotel.

Valerie said: "The killer was not much taller than me." She was 5ft 3ins. Hanratty was 5ft 8ins.

The prosecution claimed that Hanratty got himself a gun some time before the murder, although no one had ever known him own one. No evidence was produced to link him with the gun, yet it was contended that he had acquired one to become a "stick-up man," practising with it and leaving the empty cartridge cases in his room at the Vienna Hotel on the night prior to the murder. He then went to Slough to look over houses for possible burglaries – dressed in his new Hepworth suit – and ended up in a cornfield where he spotted a courting couple and was overcome by lust. It was a simple sex-murder!

Afterwards, the prosecution claimed, he went to Liverpool to fake an alibi by sending a telegram to Charles France on August 24th.

Under cross-examination in the witness-box, this question was put to Hanratty, who dismissed it with scorn.

"Are you trying to suggest to this court that I went out on August 24th to do a stick-up with a gun? Is that what you are trying to say?" he demanded.

"It is indeed."

"Well, is it not quite obvious that if I did, I would not be looking for a car in a cornfield? I would be looking for some cash, a bank, or a shop or something. If I was a stick-up man I would not bother dying my hair. I would wear a mask of some kind, because it is not your hair you have to worry about, it is your face. And if you are suggesting that I have done stick-ups, then you are wrong."

The prosecutor asked: "Do you always hold your right eyebrow higher than your left?" Hanratty replied, "I do not know, sir, because I can't see it."

Asked if he had been a professional housebreaker since the age of 16, he agreed, but reminded the jury: "This is a murder trial, not a housebreaking trial."

He went on: "The man who committed this is a maniac and a savage. I am not the kind of man the court can approve of, but I am not a maniac of any kind. I can prove it with my past girl friends. I am a decent – I cannot say honest – man, and I try to live a good and respectable life except for my housebreakings."

The prosecution introduced the evidence of a prisoner on remand in Brixton who claimed that Hanratty had confessed his guilt. But the defence produced two other prisoners who testified that the prosecution witness had never spent any time alone with Hanratty.

The cartridge cases remained a mystery. If they were planted in the hotel room, then by whom? Who knew that Hanratty had spent August 22nd at the Vienna Hotel? Charles France did. This "friend" was to prove Hanratty's downfall, turning up as a prosecution witness. He said he saw Hanratty's receipt for his hotel room and couldn't believe it cost so much.

France told the court that he put Hanratty up at his house because he felt sorry for him. Although he professed ignorance of Hanratty's housebreaking activities, he admitted advising him on the value of his hauls. He also said that the prisoner behaved very well towards Mrs. France and the couple's three children, often bringing them gifts. So what caused him to turn against this good family friend?

Hanratty once took France's 16-year-old daughter to a fair, and they petted. Hanratty told his solicitors about it before the trial, saying, "Her father would go potty if he knew."

France did just that – he went potty. Three days before the trial he was rushed to hospital after a suicide attempt, and gave his evidence flanked by two nurses.

The centrepiece of the defence case was Hanratty's Liverpool alibi. He stood by it, saying he went to Liverpool by train in the morning and spent the day of August 22nd there. His solicitors had his detailed account of his movements – he had deposited a case of stolen jewellery in the left luggage office at Lime Street Station. He described the attendant as having "a withered or turned hand." He then called at a sweet shop to ask for directions to Carlton Road. Later he tried to sell his gold watch to a man on the steps of a billiard hall.

Police were mobilised to find these people and the defence hired a private detective to help with the search. The detective found two attendants who had been on duty that day. One had fingers missing from a hand, the other an artificial arm.

In April, 1970, investigative journalist Paul Foot found the attendant with two missing fingers still at work at Lime Street left luggage office. The attendant said he had recognised Hanratty from his photograph and was sure it was the same man he had seen on August 22nd.

The police traced a Mrs. Dimwoodie, a sweetshop assistant, who also identified Hanratty from a photograph. She had only worked on August 21st and 22nd to help out, so Hanratty must have called there on one of those days. She wasn't sure which.

The police did not hand this information to the defence – it had to be prised from them. Superintendent Acott agreed that Hanratty was identified by a shopkeeper in Liverpool as having called there on August 21st or 22nd.

What were Hanratty's movements prior to the murder? At midnight on August 21st he booked into the Vienna Hotel. Earlier that day, Mrs. France testified, he had come to her home at about 2.30 p.m. "He stayed until 6.30. My daughter Carol was at home. She'd just had a tooth out. When Hanratty left he said he was going to see his old aunt in Liverpool."

A dental surgeon verified the date of Carol France's tooth extraction. If Hanratty was in London on the 21st, then his Liverpool trip must have been planned for the 22nd.

Another witness said he had seen him at the Rehearsal Club on August 21st. "His hair was black. This was not its usual colour. He left at about six or seven p.m. He told me he was going to Liverpool."

So if Hanratty did visit that Liverpool sweetshop on the 22nd, he had a cast-iron alibi. But the prosecution produced a man who said he visited the shop on the 21st and heard the lady tell of a man who had come in asking for directions to Carlton Road.

The man on the billiard hall steps was traced. He confirmed that he had been offered a gold watch, but he couldn't confirm the date beyond that it was some time in August.

The prosecution dismissed doubts about the 21st or 22nd by saying it didn't matter. Hanratty, it was rather bizarrely suggested, might have paid a "double" to go to Liverpool and fix him an alibi.

But just as the defence was building a reasonable case, Hanratty himself demolished it. On February 9th he changed his alibi. Warned by his counsel that he had to name the three Liverpool men he had gone to see, he refused to do so because they were wanted criminals. And he now told the court that he spent the night of the 22nd at Rhyl, 40 miles from Liverpool.

Yes, he had been to Liverpool, and the incidents he had spoken of were all true, but after failing to contact the three men who were his alibi, he travelled on to Rhyl to see a man called John who worked in the fairground. He'd stayed at a boarding-house for two nights, but he couldn't remember the address. He described the landlady and the boarding-house in detail, so the defence sent a private detective to Rhyl in a desperate attempt to find out if such a place existed.

Hanratty told the court that the Rhyl landlady was about 50 and wore glasses. There was a green bath in the house, and he heard trains shunting nearby.

The detective traced the landlady – a Mrs. Grace Jones. She had a green bath and she remembered Hanratty from his photograph. She said she put him up for two nights in the latter part of August, but she could not be more precise.

The prosecution produced guests who had stayed at the boarding-house at that time and none of them could remember seeing Hanratty.

Why did he change his alibi? One explanation is that at the beginning of his trial he was so confident of acquittal that he felt invincible. But when he realised how powerful a case the prosecution had against him, he was rattled. He replaced an invented alibi with the true one, thinking that the truth would save him.

He told the court: "I know I had already told Superintendent Acott a lie about Liverpool, but it was quite obvious to me that as I never committed this crime

I had nothing at all to fear. But as the case went along I got so frightened with all the evidence being brought against me, with all the lies and such things — well, it is disgraceful to talk about them. When I spoke to Mr. Acott I did not fear any danger because I knew in my heart and soul I did not commit this crime."

Superintendent Acott, in his evidence, told of an extraordinarily incriminating conversation that the prisoner had with him. Hanratty said: "You won't find my housebreakings, Mr. Acott. I never leave my fingerprints. I always rub them off with a handkerchief. I'm a really clever screwman. I never make a slip-up now. I've made over a thousand pounds in the last two months. I stick to jewellery and keep to one fence. When I came out of Manchester in March I went to see him in Ealing and he gave me twenty-five quid to start me up in business. He asked me what I was going to do now. I said, 'I think I'll pack up my jewellery lark,' and asked him to get a shooter to do some stick-ups.'"

Acott: "Are you trying to tell me you tried to get a gun from a man in Ealing?"

Hanratty: "Yes. He wouldn't play and never got me one. Oh, Mr. Acott, I've never killed a man in my life."

This reported conversation made a bad impression on the jury, but not quite so bad an impression as his change of alibi.

The jury spent nearly 10 hours deliberating before finding the prisoner guilty. Collapsing in the dock as he was sentenced to death, he cried out: "I am innocent, my lord!"

His appeal was rejected on March 13th. By then 90,000 people had signed a petition asking for a reprieve. It was not granted.

On March 16th Charles France committed suicide by gassing himself in a doss-house. At his inquest the day after Hanratty's execution, the coroner refused to reveal the contents of letters France had left, apart from saying that they were written "with great bitterness against Hanratty." So did France kill himself because he couldn't live with his guilt?

From the condemned cell Hanratty wrote to his mother: "I feel that one day my name will be cleared... I am about to take the punishment for someone else's crime." He reported in another letter that the prison governor had stopped his papers, because of the continued publicity about his case. Inside the prison he was reported as listening to the radio and talking to the officers on condemned cell duty.

Despite the belief in a number of quarters that the executioner would be hanging the wrong man, Harry Allen seemed unperturbed when he arrived at Bedford Prison with his assistant Royston Rickard on April 3rd. The gallows were housed in a separate blockhouse detached from the cellular accommodation, so unlike other establishments, Hanratty would not have to be moved away while the testing procedure took place.

The condemned man's visitors that evening included Father Keogh from Brixton Prison and Father Anthony Hulme, the Roman Catholic chaplain for Bedford Prison. Hanratty stayed awake for most of the night, writing a final letter to his parents.

Harry Allen and Royston Rickard were awake early to get to the gallows, test the drop and close the trapdoors. With everything in place, they waited until about 7.50 a.m. to be taken to the condemned cell. Among the witnesses was David Lines, the under-sheriff, who remembered the official party waiting in the execution blockhouse for Hanratty's arrival, just before eight o'clock.

Harry and his assistant waited for an officer to open the condemned cell door. They walked in on the stroke of 8 a.m. Harry pinned Hanratty's wrists behind his back and together with the chaplain and two escorting officers they left the cell and walked out into the open air to the execution blockhouse. Harry stopped Hanratty on the "T" mark across the centre of the trap-doors. Rickard applied the ankle strap and Harry placed the noose and white hood over Hanratty's head and neck. He removed the safety pins from the lever and pushed it over to release the trap-doors. Hanratty plunged through the gaping hole and died at once.

There were 300 people outside the prison but they caused no trouble. Hanratty's story did not die with him, however. During the rest of that year, 1962, Harry hanged two more men, both of whom murdered shopkeepers. Oswald Grey had killed Thomas Bates in a newsagents, James Smith murdered Isabella Cross in her shop. Meanwhile, the movement to clear Hanratty's name was beginning to gain momentum. Two parliamentary debates and numerous books and articles proclaimed that the man hanged as the A6 killer was innocent.

In 1967 Roy Jenkins, the Home Secretary, announced an investigation into the Rhyl alibi. It concluded that the alibi could not be substantiated.

Next, Peter Louis Alphon entered the picture again. He was an odd character, a drifter living on an allowance from his parents. He spent most of his time reading about witchcraft, black magic and theology. He described himself as a Fascist, with a life-long admiration for Hitler. On November 6th, 1961, he took out a writ against Superintendent Acott, alleging defamation of character and wrongful imprisonment. But he never followed it up.

Jean Justice, who wrote a book about the A6 case, says that Alphon confessed the crime to her, saying he had seen Ryan (Hanratty) at the Vienna Hotel and realised at once that he was a crook. He decided to frame him for the murder by planting the cartridge cases in Room 24 and imitating his cockney accent.

Subsequently, Fenner Brockway, MP, led a debate in the House and read transcripts from Alphon's calls to the author. After that, Alphon repeatedly confessed to the A6 murder. The framing of Hanratty had actually been done by Charles France, he said, who was paid to put the bullet cases in the hotel room and the gun under a bus seat.

In 1967 Alphon called a press conference in Paris and told assembled newsmen that a wealthy London businessman had paid him a large sum of money to end the relationship between Gregsten and Valerie Storie.

"Another man then put a gun in my hand. I gave the couple in the car two chances to go away. I sent him away twice, but each time the bloody man came back." (This was a reference to Gregsten leaving the car to go to the milk dispenser and later to the cigarette machine.)

The authorities took the view that Alphon was a mentally ill publicity-seeker. His story was remarkably detailed and fitted the psychological pattern of the crime, but it was too like an attempt by a novelist to get inside the mind of the killer. While convincing as a narrative, it was weak on proof.

Alphon confessed, retracted, confessed again until few took him seriously. But his antics kept the case in the public eye. Many had doubts about the safety of the conviction.

Then came the introduction of DNA "fingerprinting." This new scientific tool could not only solve mysteries of the present – it could also reach back to the grave to crack unsolved and disputed crimes of the past.

Preserved on the underwear Valerie Storie wore at the time of the murder was semen from the man who killed her lover and then raped her. Thanks to DNA that semen could now signpost Gregsten's killer.

Confident that such a test would at last clear their hanged relative, the Hanratty family pressed for it to be applied. The case was reinvestigated, and for a start James Hanratty's 59-year-old brother Michael gave a saliva sample for DNA comparison with samples on Valerie's preserved underwear.

In 1997 the *Daily Mirror*'s story that Hanratty was set to be cleared was welcomed by his relieved family. It was understood that the DNA findings would not be contested in the law courts and the conviction would be quashed. Michael said the development was long overdue. "I only wish my father, and James, were here to share this with us," he said. "We just want his name cleared. That is all we live for."

All that seemed right and fair, except that it carried along with it the belief that the DNA would prove Hanratty innocent. It did the opposite – it proved him guilty.

The sample on the underwear showed a match with samples taken from Hanratty's relatives. The results were short of the 100 per cent match required to make the tests conclusive, but comparison with samples taken from Hanratty's remains would put the match beyond doubt. The Court of Appeal consequently authorised an exhumation.

Hanratty's body had been removed from Bedford Prison and re-buried with a family funeral at Carpenters Park, near Watford, on February 22nd, 1966. There it stayed until 2001, when it was exhumed and fragments of the bones were tested.

The results were announced in the Appeal Court on May 10th, 2002. "The DNA evidence establishes beyond doubt that James Hanratty was the murderer," Lord Woolf, the Lord Chief Justice, told the court. "The DNA evidence makes what was a strong case even stronger." The court rejected all 17 grounds of appeal brought by Hanratty's family and friends.

Some continued to argue. They claim that DNA evidence could be flawed, and it would be only a matter of time before it was successfully challenged. There was already proof that two people could have the same DNA. But these were straws in the wind. There is an overwhelming case that Hanratty was the A6 killer. His remains have been reburied, and reburied too should now be any lingering doubts about his conviction.

CHAPTER 9

DORIS

Harry was a divorced man living alone when he met Doris Dyke, who was to become his second wife. She had worked in the National Coal Board laboratory for 10 years and, looking for something a bit more independent, took hairdressing lessons. She started her own salon and one night she went out with friends to Harry's pub.

"The friends wanted to buy a pub of their own, and the likeliest person for them to ask about it was Harry Allen," she remembered "I'd never met him before – I just went along for the night out. He struck me as very jolly.

"That night he came with us to the pub my friends were interested in acquiring. They talked about it and on Harry's advice they decided not to buy it. We all went on to a club and later he took me across to another pub, one he used to own. He introduced me to a few people, saying, 'This lady is going to be my wife. We're getting married.' I thought it was very funny. I didn't know him from Adam, but I was quite flattered because he had all these women flocking around him."

They were married within the year, in October, 1963, and for Doris, at the age of 39, it was a new experience because she had never been married before. Harry's two children were already grown up – Brian was married with a child of his own and Christine was 17.

After the wedding bells Doris gave up hairdressing to help out Harry in his new pub, the Woodman Inn at Middleton. She says: "I think the reason we got married so quickly was that he was changing pubs. He was going to a new pub and he wanted to go in as a married man. I told my mother that I had known him for years. That was a little white lie, of course."

Many years later Harry was to say, "Doris is a real

treasure. She has never discussed my work as hangman, although I know she is in favour of the death penalty."

Interestingly, a regular customer at the Woodman Inn was a Manchester man named Dennis Murtagh. He had been convicted of the murder of William Jackson by running him over in his car. Dennis Murtagh spent 13 weeks in the condemned cell at Strangeways Prison. His execution date was set for April 1st, 1955, with Harry Allen engaged as assistant to Albert Pierrepoint. But Murtagh's conviction was quashed on appeal and he was freed. What better place, then, for him to take his evening drink than in the pub of the man who might have participated in his hanging?

Murtagh and Harry became good friends. Murtagh asked Harry to be best man at his wedding, but mine host at the Woodman politely refused. To have your potential hangman as your best man would, he thought, "have been in bad taste." But the two men regularly chatted in the bar and laughed about the way that fate had brought them together.

One thing that Harry's new wife Doris was certain about – she had no idea at the time she married him that he also had a job as a hangman. Even when he did tell her she shrugged – as far as she was concerned he was still Harry the publican and she was his wife working in the bar.

"No sooner had we returned from our honeymoon than he had to go off to a hanging in Bristol. I must admit, I wondered what his mood would be like when he returned. I needn't have worried. He was just the same old Harry."

Harry's reticence to talk about his job extended to his son Brian. During his National Service Brian was called before his C.O. and was told that he couldn't be posted to Germany with the rest of his unit because of his father's job.

"My father's job?" Brian asked, somewhat perplexed.

"Well, yes," said the C.O. "You see, Albert Pierrepoint hanged quite a few Germans in Germany in his career and it's thought that if you go to Germany and the local people find out who you are there might be some adverse reaction."

"But why?" a bewildered Brian asked. "What has all this got to do with me? My father isn't Albert Pierrepoint, he's Harry Allen."

"Yes, Harry Allen the hangman," replied the C.O. That was the first time Brian Allen learned about his father's other job. If that sounds astonishing, imagine what an effect it must have had at that precise moment in the C.O's office! Brian didn't go to Germany – instead he was posted to Korea.

Even after Doris and Harry were married, he didn't talk much about the other job. "Well, sometimes, he did perhaps," Doris recalls. "He was always very.... Well, he would go only so far with people. He was always joking. If you went anywhere and heard someone laughing, Harry would be in the middle of it. He was absolutely brimming over with personality. I just sat in the background and listened."

There was a bit of gallows humour, though, if only in the bar, where a notice was prominently displayed: "No hanging round the bar."

Doris in fact met Harry for the first time when he was almost at the end of his career as a hangman. "It didn't come into my life really, him being a hangman. After I married him there were only two more hangings." These were the executions of Russell Pascoe on December 17th, 1963, and of Gwynne Owen Evans on August 13th, 1964.

But with 27 down and only two to go in his capacity as chief executioner, she still remembers the nightmare of dealing with the press.

"They harassed us terribly. They would come into the pub and sit here all day. On an execution day the police would come in plain clothes too and sit in the bar, and you couldn't tell them from the reporters. I suppose the police were there to protect Harry. Anyway, I would start chatting with the reporters, and then in the paper the following day there would be things said which I hadn't said. They twisted everything. And when the capital punishment debates began in Parliament we were inundated with them.

"There was one reporter who came here – her name was Susan. She was well known on television. She came in and had a whisky, and so did Harry. She was trying to get Harry drunk, which was a complete waste of time because he could hold his drink. I'd never seen him drunk. This woman Susan – she was getting drunk instead. Her language was atrocious.

"She kept getting on the phone and saying, 'Oh, I'll find out, I'll find out.' I won't repeat some of the other things she said – it's too terrible for a woman. So in the end I got a bit fed up and said to Harry, 'Get rid of her.' That's what he eventually did.

"There was a parliamentary debate on about capital punishment, you see, and she was trying to find out what Harry thought about it. She came back the next day too, when we had a friend come to see us. Every time we talked to our friend this Susan kept barging in. Harry controlled himself as long as he could but in the end he just asked her to leave. Oh, they were terrible!

"I didn't know much about the executions, to be honest. He didn't get nervous or anything like that before a hanging. It was just a normal job for him. It didn't bother him at all. If he told me anything at all, it was usually a bit of trivia. Like the woman pathologist who after the execution put her briefcase between the dead man's legs and went on writing up her report."

Doris and Harry used to frequent the Prison Club in Strangeways. Sometimes they saw Albert Pierrepoint there. "But I didn't speak to him much," Doris remembers. "He and Harry had their differences. He asked Harry for a loan and Harry refused – so after that they didn't bother with each other."

It was in 1952 that their relationship had soured. The pair had met up at Wandsworth Prison to discuss rope design on 2nd or 3rd of April and it was then that Pierrepoint asked Harry for some money. When Harry refused, I was reliably informed, Pierrepoint's somewhat dramatic response was to take a rope out of his briefcase and say, "Well, it looks as if I'll have to sell this then." The dates would certainly match up as the pair did meet at Wandsworth to discuss rope design at that time. The mention of Pierrepoint caused Doris to groan... "Oh, that film!"

"That film" was the Pierrepoint film, and Doris positively loathed it. It was, she says, "absolute rubbish," and "boring," and "terrible."

"Pierrepoint would never have worn a cardigan, for instance, he just wasn't a cardigan type. And as for the bit where they suggest that after the execution the hangman washes the body, it's totally untrue."

She is right, of course. I was advising on set at the making of the movie *Pierrepoint* and the body-washing scene astonished me. I asked the producers where on earth they got that idea from, but no one took any notice.

The idea put across in the film that Pierrepoint was emotionally affected by the number of hangings he had to perform in Germany was, says Doris, so much nonsense. Pierrepoint was a "cocky" man, but a "jolly" man too. And Mrs. Pierrepoint was "a lovely person."

Doris feels badly about the lack of official recognition that came Harry's way when he finally retired. "He was ruled body and soul by the Home Office," she says. "He couldn't say anything that they might object to. I actually have a letter from the Home Office, which is a reply to his request for permission to write his memoirs. The Home Office said, yes, you can write something about your life, but you must not refer to your official duties. So who wants to know about being a publican?"

Talking to Doris I got the impression that even a book about Harry the publican might be interesting. For, even though she is probably slightly partisan, Harry Allen comes across as a man of extraordinary kindness and good nature. Doris says, "There was a couple who used to come into the pub who had a daughter with a disability. She couldn't talk, she couldn't do anything, her body was all twisted. But Harry always made a fuss of her. She would be slavering, but he would kiss her on the cheek.

"He could talk to anyone, from up there to down here. The scruffiest, the roughest – he could always somehow get through to them. On Sundays he used to take all the lads out to the Prison Club. They'd have a session there, and then they'd all go back to the pub."

Harry Allen was one of those life-loving men who left the stamp of his remarkable personality on everyone he met. Doris, who was married to him for 30 years, remembers they were "sufficient for each other." The only thing that irked was that he wouldn't go abroad for holidays. "At least, not while he was working," she says. "But after he retired I finally persuaded him."

CHAPTER 10

THE CORNER SHOP MURDERS

Six months had gone by since the hanging of James Hanratty when Harry was summoned to Birmingham Prison for another execution. The long countdown to abolition was already beginning. He had already hanged the last man to be executed in London; now this hanging was to be the last ever at Birmingham's Winson Green Prison.

This was to be another case mired in controversy and as such another nail in the coffin of capital punishment.

If murder can be described as simple, this was simple enough. Newsagent Thomas Bates had put in a long day at his shop, which was just around the corner from Birmingham's Edgbaston cricket ground. Now, at 6.30 p.m., he was thinking about closing time. The last-minute rush of schoolboys that sometimes happened, to buy the "pink-un" for the latest county cricket scores, hadn't occurred that day, and Mr. Bates was feeling tired.

He served the last few customers, and did not seem to notice that one of them, a short, slightly built black man who had dropped behind the others, was wearing a handkerchief over the lower part of his face. A second or two later the customers had gone, leaving only the man with the handkerchief on his face.

The man pulled out a gun, mumbled something incoherent, and fired. A single shot rang out. Mr. Bates let out a sharp cry and grabbed the left side of his chest.

As he slumped over the counter, blood splashed over the last of the evening papers. The gunman, apparently panic-stricken, turned at once and fled from the shop empty-handed.

Thomas Bates, 47 and unmarried, lived above his

shop in Lea Bank Road with his 79-year-old mother Louisa Bates. When she heard the gunshot, her son's cry, and the subsequent crash, she called out. Getting no reply, she hurried into the shop, and at the sight of her son lying in a pool of blood, she rushed out into the street calling for help. But Thomas Bates was already beyond all human aid.

As Birmingham Police descended on the tragic little newsagent's, they had reasons enough to be puzzled. The shop was a world away from the inner city areas of Soho and Lozells, which, by 1962, were showing signs of serious industrial decline and increasing violent crime. Edgbaston was definitely not the kind of place where you would expect a shopkeeper to be murdered.

Then again, what could possibly be the motive for such a murder? It had to be robbery, yet nothing was taken. Did Mrs. Bates' shout from above scare off the intended thief? Or was he simply frightened by the enormity of what he had done?

In the hunt for witnesses the police threw a huge dragnet over the city. Who were those last few customers in Mr. Bates' shop on Thursday, June 2nd, 1962? Could they identify the last customer, the man with a gun in his hand?

The hunt did not last long. One by one the witnesses came forward and the search was narrowed down to a West Indian man. Systematically, the police raided a number of districts in Birmingham with large West Indian populations.

More than 200 men were detained for questioning and as they told their stories one name came up again and again. He was Oswald Augustus Grey, a 20-year-old unemployed Jamaican baker. Grey, it transpired, was destitute and had been receiving unemployment benefits for more than a year.

A 24-hour watch was posted on him and it soon proved fruitful. The surveillance team saw him reach into a dustbin near his home. They swooped, and found him in the act of pocketing bullets. He was taken to the police station and questioned. There he admitted possessing the murder weapon, but said he had had it for only a short time and only on two different occasions – at 3.30 on the afternoon of the shooting and later at 10 p.m.

The tenor of his argument was that someone else was in possession of it between those times, which included the time of the murder. Then he made a written statement in which he gave five different stories as to who had the gun at the time of the murder. The police, having no doubt at all who did actually have it, charged Oswald Grey with the murder. But where was the murder weapon?

While Grey was held for weeks in custody an intensive search was conducted, but the murder weapon was never found.

Oswald Grey was brought before Birmingham Assizes in October where he pleaded not guilty. Prosecution witnesses told the court of seeing him in the vicinity of Thomas Bates' shop between 6.30 and 6.45 p.m. Ballistics experts who examined the bullets taken from Grey at the time of his arrest determined that a similar bullet had killed Mr. Bates, although it could not be proved that it was exactly the same.

Grey, giving evidence on his own behalf, claimed that at no time during the afternoon of June 2nd was he in Lea Bank Road, nor did he accept the view of prosecution witnesses who said they saw him standing at the corner of Lea Bank Road by the barber shop, and sitting in the Black and White café.

He agreed he stole a revolver from a friend's room, but said he did so because another man asked him to get a gun. He did not tell the police this because he wanted to shield the other man.

The man who was in possession of the gun at the time Mr. Bates was shot, Grey claimed, was another West Indian, named Karnif Mover. Earlier, Mover, giving evidence as a prosecution witness, claimed that he never had the gun at any time.

Grey later sold the gun for £16 to a man at a party in Burbury Street. Next day he returned to Balsall Heath to collect some more bullets he had hidden in a dustbin and was arrested by the police.

On the way to the police station, Grey said, the officers spat at him and kicked him, and told him it would be best to confess. At the police station he claimed, "they gave me the third degree," beating him and causing him to make statements he now regretted.

He agreed that when the prison doctor examined him he did not mention the bruises to his ankles, which, he claimed, were made by the police, because he did not consider them serious enough.

The prosecution were sufficiently concerned about Grey's allegations of police maltreatment for Mr. Graham Swanwick QC, for the Crown, to call Detective Chief Superintendent Gerald Baumber. Told of the prisoner's allegations, Baumber replied, "There is no truth whatever in them."

He was asked: "Did the accused man appear to you, when you saw him, to be in physical fear of the police?"

"Not at all," replied Chief Superintendent Baumber.

Grey did not appear to have any pain or to have any injuries inflicted on him. Nor did he complain of any sort of ill-treatment or intimidation.

Chief Inspector Benbow corroborated Chief Superintendent Baumber's evidence. Cross-examined by Mr. A. E. James QC, defending, Benbow said he did not tell the accused man that he had to admit the charge, nor did he spit at him.

Mr. James: "I suggest you hit the accused?"

"No. That never happened."

Two other police officers were called to refute Grey's allegations. The defence then called four women to say that Grey was not the man they saw near the scene of the shooting.

Anna Maria Scott from Ladywood said she saw a black man, but he was not the prisoner. The man she saw was taller and had a thin face and sunken cheeks.

Annette Evans from Edgbaston said she saw a black man inside the newsagent's shop at 6.20 and she left him there when she came out. The man seemed anxious for her to be served first, but when he was served he quickly rushed out. He was 5ft 10in tall, well built and had straight hair, whereas Grey had curly hair.

Mrs. Marion Beatrice Woolley from Great Colmore Street said she saw a black man looking to see if the road was clear. He then took a handkerchief out of his pocket, fastened it behind his head and pulled it down. Then he walked back towards the newsagent's shop, which he entered "at about 6.25."

She thought the man was "acting stupidly." He was 35 to 40 years old and had hollow cheeks. He looked ill, desperate and hungry. This man was not Oswald Grey.

Her daughter Carole Woolley corroborated her story.

Mr. Swanwick, for the Crown, told the jury that the damning evidence against Grey was his own knowledge that the gun in his possession was stolen, that it was used in the shooting, and that he admitted having it on several occasions during the day that Mr. Bates was killed.

Describing the kind of atmosphere in which the Jamaican lived, he said: "We are moving in a rather strange world. We are among people who steal guns, who traffic in guns, people who live rather aimless lives in nightclubs and dives. We are among people whose abodes shift from place to place, sharing rooms, sometimes with one and sometimes with another, sometimes sleeping with prostitutes, sometimes sharing rooms with other men. It is a strange, fluctuating world."

The judge made special reference to the complaint of maltreatment by Grey during his summing-up. "This man says the police knocked him about, kicked him, hit him and spat at him, and that it was because of this treatment that he said what he did to the police. If you think this is true – if you think the police did ill-treat him and that they got statements from him by ill-treating him – then I tell you at once, pay not the slightest attention to the statements.

"Of course the police say his complaint is quite

untrue, but it is for you to judge between the police and the accused. But I am bound to tell you this. It is very easy for a man who has made a damaging statement to come to court and to say: 'I was ill-treated.'

"You saw Chief Superintendent Baumber in the box. Mr. Swanwick, for the Crown, sat down without asking him what the accused said when he was charged.

"Now, what the accused said when he was charged was very much in his favour, and it was Chief Superintendent Baumber who reminded counsel about this. I was struck by that. If you think that Chief Superintendent Baumber is that sort of man, it is a little difficult to think that he allowed this man to be ill-treated in front of him."

The judge advised the jury to be careful of any eyewitness evidence, particularly the evidence of the prosecution witness Karnif Mover.

The jury took only 50 minutes to find Oswald Grey guilty and he was sentenced to hang. It took only another 15 minutes for the Appeal Court to dismiss Grey's plea that there was no direct evidence of him having shot Mr. Bates.

Indeed, Mr. James, Grey's counsel, addressing the judges, said he could produce no constructive argument against conviction. He told the appeal judges: "The evidence supports the jury's verdict. I cannot point to any misdirection in the judge's summing-up."

Lord Parker, the Lord Chief Justice, agreed. The motive of robbery could be properly implied, although it did not take place. Since the defendant had pleaded not guilty, no questions of manslaughter or insanity were at issue. The jury had a simple task of deciding if Grey killed Mr. Bates.

Lord Parker said the judge's summing-up was more than fair to Grey. Two indicators as to Grey's guilt particularly struck the appeal judges: his constant lying and his arrest with other bullets from the murder weapon.

The appeal was dismissed. Oswald Grey is said to have spent his last six weeks on earth limbo-dancing and hand-jiving in the death cell, apparently indifferent to his fate.

Four Birmingham University students holding up anti-capital punishment slogans stood in silence outside the prison as the execution hour drew near. Eight uniformed officers and four plainclothes policemen guarded them.

Was Grey as guilty as he superficially sounds? This was Britain in the 1960s, remember, when the first wave of immigrants were settling down in a climate of some hostility. The British way of life, and of doing things, was new and foreign to them. Oswald Grey might have been bewildered by the events following his arrest. He would have been the only black man in the police station, possibly the only black man on remand; white lawyers and white policemen would have surrounded him. He would have been in an alien world.

So the newsagent's last customer became the last man hanged at Birmingham's Winson Green Prison, on October 12th, 1962. As Harry Allen put on his bowler hat after the hanging he was not to know that only three years now remained before the abolition of capital punishment.

•

Harry's next execution, the following month, involved another corner shop murder. It was discovered by nine-year-old Stephanie Howard when, skipping happily to her Auntie Bella's sweetshop in Hulme Hall Lane, Miles Platting, Manchester, she was surprised not to find her aunt at the counter to greet her.

The child waited a moment, and then peeped anxiously behind the counter. Her aunt, Mrs. Isabella Cross, the shop's 57-year-old proprietor, was lying on the floor, her blue overall pulled over her head.

Returning to the home of her married sister, a few streets away, Stephanie burst in, crying: "Auntie Bella's dying!" Her sister hurried to the sweetshop, accompanied by a friend. Stephanie had not exaggerated. Isabella Cross was dead.

Stephanie had arrived at the shop at 4.30 p.m. on May 4th, 1962. Fifteen minutes later the police were on the scene. They found that Isabella Cross had been battered to death, her attacker beating her about the head with five fizzy drink bottles. Fragments of glass from the bottles were strewn over the floor.

Neighbours were soon able to suggest a motive. Mrs. Cross and her husband were known to have tickets for the Cup Final. It was common knowledge that the couple planned to go to London next day to see their team, Burnley, play at Wembley. Consequently, Isabella's elderly mother, who lived with the couple, had already gone to stay with another daughter. Possibly the killer knew of the mother's absence and therefore chose that particular day for the attack.

Well, it was a theory. But Mr. Cross, summoned home from his work at the Royal Ordnance factory at Patricroft, told detectives that he had the Cup Final tickets safely in his jacket pocket. And there was plenty of evidence that what the attacker was after was money – all the cash had gone from the shop's open till, and a few coins were scattered on the floor.

Open, bloodstained drawers were found in the living-room behind the shop. An unsuccessful attempt had been made to force the locked drawers of a desk, and the killer had apparently left by the back door, which bore traces of blood, as did the back yard gate.

Two days before the murder, Isabella's husband was redecorating. On the edge of the recently painted door to the living-room, police found three fingerprints. They were not those of Mr. Cross, Isabella, her mother or any friends or relatives.

Shortly after the murder, detectives stopped a man they noticed loitering near the Crosses' back yard. Fragments of glass were embedded in the soles of his shoes. Taken to police headquarters, the man admitted killing the shopkeeper, but his fingerprints did not match those found on the door and he was swiftly eliminated from the investigation. He was a crank, the police decided, and was simply seeking notoriety for a crime he didn't commit.

Three weeks passed before detectives got the lead they were looking for. Officers in Edinburgh produced a match for the fingerprints found on Isabella's living-room door. The prints were those of James Smith, a 26-year-old former Edinburgh man with a criminal record. When he moved down to Manchester he found work as a rubber moulder in Failsworth.

Police mounted a round-the-clock watch on his home in Corfe Street, Beswick, while other inquiries established that Smith was in the process of moving house and had already sold some of his furniture.

His shift at the firm of Ferguson Shiers on May 4th had finished at midday, and one of his colleagues told detectives that he had accompanied Smith to a local pub that lunchtime. After having a drink, the workmate left Smith at about 2.45 p.m. This was a deviation from their routine – they usually caught a bus home together, and Smith would alight at the junction of Oldham Road and Hulme Hall Lane, near the Crosses' shop.

Two days after the murder, Smith called at his workmate's home. His colleague noticed a piece of sticking plaster on Smith's right hand. Smith said he had cut himself on a spike in his back yard.

The police had heard enough. At 8 a.m. on May 6th, they knocked on Smith's door. It was opened by a tall, slim man who stared hard at the officers.

"Yes," he admitted. "I am James Smith."

Inside the house the suspect was joined by his wife, their baby and two stepchildren.

"Do you know the sweetshop in Hulme Hall Lane?" asked one of the detectives. Smith said he did.

Had he walked past the shop on May 4th?

"Yes, I walked past the shop on my way home that day, but I never entered the premises," he replied.

Arrested and charged with the murder of Isabella Cross, he said: "I was drinking at a pub near my work until 4 p.m., then I went straight home. At 4.30 an insurance collector called at my house, so I paid him and he left."

The insurance agent confirmed that he called at the Smith house that day, but said he arrived at 4.45 p.m., and he could not remember whether Smith was there or not.

Police established that Isabella Cross was murdered between 4.20 p.m., when a cigarette delivery was made at the shop, and 4.30 p.m., when her body was discovered. Smith could have committed the crime, with enough time to complete the 12-minute walk home before the insurance man arrived.

Asked how his fingerprints came to be on Mrs. Cross's living-room door, Smith remained silent.

Searching his home, police went to work on his settee with a vacuum cleaner. As the dust was sucked up from the side of one of the cushions, a tiny fragment of glass was collected. It was sent to the forensic science laboratory near Preston for examination.

That settee was up for sale together with Smith's other furniture. Had it already been sold, what turned out to be a vital piece of evidence might have been lost forever.

James Smith's four-day trial began at Liverpool Crown Court on October 14th, 1962. He pleaded not guilty, but the jury preferred to believe the evidence of the fingerprints and that telltale fragment of glass.

In his summing-up the judge paid tribute to the work of the forensic team involved in the case. More than 200 man-hours were spent on painstakingly gluing together the pieces of those shattered fizzy drink bottles that had been the murder weapon. It was time well spent.

Convicted and sentenced to death, Smith assured his wife that he would not hang. His appearance, however, belied his confidence. His 6ft 2in frame shrank visibly as the weeks passed, and his brown hair turned white.

Harry Allen arrived at Strangeways Prison in the afternoon of November 27th, accompanied by his assistant John Underhill. At 8 a.m. next day they led

James Smith from the condemned cell to the scaffold and hanged him.

Nine months passed before Harry was back on duty. In 1963 he hanged only two men – fewer than in any other year. The first was on August 15th, when he executed Henry John Burnett, found guilty of killing Thomas Guyon on July 25th that same year. Burnett had been having an affair with Guyon's wife.

Harry flew to Scotland for the execution at Aberdeen Prison. The gallows he operated there was the most modern in Britain, because it had been built only the year previously. Burnett turned out to be the last man executed in Scotland. There would be just one more execution that year, and perhaps for Harry that was just as well, for he was about to have a new wife and a new pub to occupy his time.

Two months after executing Henry Burnett, Harry married Doris Dyke in the Methodist church in Astley village, near Leigh. When his divorce from Marjorie came through the previous year he was heard to say, "I don't think I will ever marry again," which of course is what a lot of twice-married men say after their first marriage is dissolved.

Photographers and sightseers crowded the entrance to the little church, but police turned out to move them gently on. There was a police guard too, at the reception at a Leigh restaurant.

Bride and groom moved immediately into the Woodman Inn at Middleton, along with Buster, Harry's boxer dog. This was the second time the town had had an executioner-landlord. Many years before public executioner Arthur Ellis was mine host at the Jolly Butcher.

As he pulled his first pints at the Woodman, Harry said: "This and my other job don't mix. I refuse to discuss it with customers. There are plenty of other things to talk about."

The local paper described the new landlord as "pleasant and approachable," and "looking like a businessman in a dark striped suit, white shirt and quiet blue tie. He has a neat moustache." The outgoing licensee described him as "a jolly nice fellow."

Harry said: "I like Middleton. I've been 30 years in the licensing trade and I've been in several big pubs. I was looking for somewhere quieter and when I heard the Woodman was on the market I applied for it. I'm looking forward to settling down in the town. I already know one or two people here."

Harry's second and final execution of that year, 1963, involved a cold-blooded killer whose victim's story must surely be among the most bizarre in criminal annals.

•

For nearly 40 years William Garfield Rowe's Cornish farming family persuaded the rest of the world that he was dead.

The events that shaped his astonishing life began in 1917 when at the age of 18 he left his family's farm in Porthleven, Cornwall, to join the Royal Artillery. Rowe was not the sort of stuff that volunteers were made of – he had to be conscripted to fight for king and country because he detested all forms of violence. It took him less than a week to decide that army life wasn't for him, so he simply deserted and returned home to the farm. There he re-joined his two younger brothers and got on with ploughing the fields and bringing in the cows, just as if the unfortunate military interlude had never occurred.

The army, however, didn't allow that sort of thing to happen. When the military police came looking for him, Rowe hid in a cupboard. But aware that they would almost certainly return, and that next time they might find him, he decided to leave home. He had no set plan – he would roam the countryside, supported by the £50 his fond mother gave him.

Within a month his luck ran out. He was arrested in Gloucester, court-martialled for desertion and sent to an army detention camp on the Isle of Wight. The army, however, were reckoning without their prisoner's homing instinct. Rowe promptly escaped and soon afterwards his family were not at all surprised when he walked back through the front door of their farmhouse.

Rowe was a wanted man and he realised that he had only exchanged one form of imprisonment for another. He could only remain free by hiding out at the farm during the day and emerging at night. This would be his plan for the future, and he was fully supported by his parents and his brothers, who blandly assured the military police each time they called that William had completely disappeared, and as far as they were concerned he had gone off to be a soldier.

Then, in 1918, a year after William's call-up, the war ended.

So would William now be coming home a hero, the neighbours inquired? No, replied his dispirited parents. He wouldn't be coming home because he had been killed in action.

For the next 39 years, as far as the rest of the world was concerned, William Rowe was a dead man, lying in some poppy-covered grave in northern France. And for the next 39 years there were curious happenings at the Venta Vedna farm, owned by the Rowe family.

Neighbours noticed that each time William's father and brothers finished work for the day, somehow their labours appeared to be augmented overnight. At dusk the trio would return to their farmhouse after a day spent cutting and binding corn. But by dawn the corn would be revealed to have been miraculously stacked. Similarly, carts left empty at nightfall were loaded with vegetables at dawn next day.

Not for one moment could anyone have imagined that this was all the work of William working under cover of darkness. After all, everyone knew William was dead.

The farm, declared the superstitious locals, must be pixie-blessed. There could be no other explanation.

But if the pixies came at night, they wondered, how come the house was always locked so securely when the family was out in the fields all day? This wasn't a crime area – in fact, crime didn't exist in Porthleven. The neighbours put this eccentricity down to the family's bereavement. The war had left many folk with strange ways.

Then came the Second World War, presenting the Rowes with new problems. They couldn't apply for a ration book or clothing coupons for their eldest son, because as far as the rest of the world was concerned he didn't exist. But he had to eat and be clothed like everyone else.

The problem was partially solved by the farm produce, which kept William fed. As for his clothes, it wasn't as if he was going anywhere, and there was no one to set eyes on him apart from his parents and his two brothers. Dressing up was not a priority for an invisible man, and William was quite happy with his brothers' hand-me-downs He would wear anything as long as it wasn't khaki – which, after 1917, he'd sworn never to wear again.

During the war his brother Joel had married and moved away from Venta Vedna farm. In 1949 his father died and, unable to attend the funeral, William watched the procession from a hiding-place in the hayloft. The farm, which would ordinarily have become his, was left to his brother Stanley.

Stanley decided that the time had come for the family to move to a better farm, and it seems that the one he settled for was chosen with William in mind. It was called Nanjarrow, near the Wendron Moors. It was remote and isolated, and the only approach was by way of a cart track more than a mile long. It was the perfect spot for an invisible man.

On moving day William made the journey concealed under a pile of sacks at the bottom of a farm wagon driven by Stanley.

In 1954 Stanley died, leaving everything to his mother, who now ran the farm during the daytime, with William taking over at night.

Suddenly, a light appeared in William's dark world. The government decided to grant a royal pardon to the deserters of both world wars. At 57 William Rowe was born again – he could live like other men at last.

Well, not quite like other men. Four decades during which he had been shut away from the rest of the world, living in constant fear of discovery, had made William unlike other men. He had developed the habits of a nervous recluse, and he couldn't shake them off. When his mother died a year later, able to leave him everything, he continued to live almost as he had always lived – a creature of the night who slept by day.

Although he now had the means to go anywhere, to go out and enjoy himself, he had known no other woman than his mother, and for 39 years his only male company had been that of his father and two brothers.

Going out in fact required an effort of will he detested. Occasionally he drove his farm cart to cattle markets, and to Constantine, the nearest village, to buy groceries and household necessities. And wherever he went he paid cash. William distrusted banks and post offices, and believed only in banknotes and coins.

"He's really a very wealthy miser," the rumour ran. "Up at Nanjarrow he's got a small fortune stashed away…"

So it was inevitable that William came back one day from a cattle market to find his farmhouse ransacked. The thieves had made off with cash and jewellery worth £200. Detectives surveying the scene advised him to put his money and his valuables into a bank for safekeeping. William shook his head. He would just have to find better hiding places in the house.

His only visitor from time to time was Joel, his surviving brother. Joel found him living happily enough, running the farm with occasional outside help and doing his own cooking and housework, although that was rudimentary. He noticed that William used none of the four bedrooms in the house, preferring to sleep on a couch in the sitting-room. And William was still a great reader.

At 64 William was fit and vigorous. He had gradually got used to working by day and sleeping by night, so every morning he was up at dawn to tend his cattle, and he always put in a full day's work on the farm. The evenings and the nights he spent alone, but he had been alone for too much of his life to suffer from loneliness.

So it was with some surprise that he looked up from his book at around 11 p.m. on Wednesday, August 14th, 1963, at the sound of someone knocking on the door. He was immediately worried. No one ever called at this time of night. Because he was a man who had always abhorred violence, he kept no guns in the house. If the caller was aggressive, William was virtually defenceless. He moved slowly to the door and opened it cautiously.

Two young men, one wearing what appeared to be a motorbike helmet, stood on the doorstep.

"My friend here is a helicopter pilot," announced the helmeted man's companion. "He was taking me to the airport at Land's End when the engine conked out. Then we saw your light."

William had just time enough to digest this before he saw that one of the callers was holding a small crowbar and the other had a knife in his hand.

Next morning, a cattle dealer from Truro, responding to a phone call William had made several days previously from a shop in the village, offering two cows for sale, arrived at Nanjarrow Farm. The dealer had got to know William reasonably well in recent years, and was one of the few locals on friendly terms with him. Driving his wagon into the farmyard he sounded his horn, knowing that he was expected and imagining that the farmer would appear any minute.

But there was no sign of William. Perplexed, the cattle dealer went to the farm's front door, which was swinging open. He pushed his way in and gasped in dismay. The inside of the house was in a state of complete turmoil – the contents of drawers were strewn over the floors, a couch was slashed, furniture overturned.

The dealer ran upstairs, calling William by name. There was no sign of the farmer but plenty more evidence that the place had been thoroughly ransacked.

Mattresses were ripped open, their stuffing littering the bedrooms.

The dealer ran downstairs and ran to his wagon, intending to fetch the police. He was about to climb on when he saw a trail of blood on the ground. Following it to an outhouse he found William Rowe's body. The farmer had been murdered – bludgeoned and repeatedly stabbed in the chest.

Officers from Constantine called to the scene found that William Rowe's wallet, in his pocket, was empty. A paraffin lamp was still burning in the living-room of the farmhouse, indicating that the attack had occurred at night.

The post-mortem established that the victim had first been stunned by a blow to the head and then stabbed five times with a long-bladed knife. Bloodstains suggested that he had been struck down by the back door, and that his body was then dragged to the outhouse in a hasty attempt at concealment. But there was no quick way to establish whether anything was stolen.

The local police decided to call in Scotland Yard, and Detective Superintendent Maurice Osborne and Detective Sergeant Andrew McPhee arrived from London. Two fingerprint experts and a forensic scientist joined them from Bristol.

Neither the murder weapons nor any clear fingerprints were found, but something of the victim's lifestyle and habits soon emerged.

"Whenever he owed me money, he would excuse himself and go into another room," said the cattle dealer. "He would come out with the cash, usually in pound notes or fivers. I've no idea where he had the money hidden, but he seemed to have plenty of it and he didn't have far to go to get it."

Joel Rowe, William's brother, first heard the news on the radio, and went to the farm to tell detectives that his brother had inherited at least several thousand pounds, in addition to the valuable property.

"He died twice," Joel explained to the police. "The first time was back in 1917. He let the world pass him by during the good years of his life. Seven years ago he came to life again, a rich man. But by then he was too old, at least he thought he was. He died a second time, horribly, without ever having learned to live."

Where had William hidden his money? Joel had no idea, so Superintendent Osborne ordered a thorough search of the farmhouse. In a short time a detective retrieved an odd-looking document from among papers littering the living-room floor. The papers apparently came from a drawer in the victim's desk, and the document that intrigued the investigators was handwritten in Esperanto and appeared to be a list.

A Helston solicitor familiar with Esperanto was called in to translate.

"It's a list of various locations, probably hiding-places, around the house and property," he explained. "A certain brick in the fireplace, the base of a paraffin lamp, an old coat in the attic, a can buried outdoors near a rose bush."

With this information, the officers discovered more than £3,000. The killers were obviously unaware of the significance of the document they had dumped on the floor. Superintendent Osborne had already made up his mind that there was more than one intruder – the victim's injuries proved that two weapons were used.

By examining tyre tracks in the lane they deduced that a motorbike that was left about 100 yards short of the house had recently approached the farmhouse. Convinced that the killers must be local – who else would know of remote Nanjarrow Farm and its owner's rumoured wealth? – Superintendent Osborne compiled a list of all known motorbike owners in west Cornwall. Detectives questioned all of them – but none aroused any suspicions.

One, however, had yet to be interviewed. His name was Russell Pascoe, 23, and when officers went to his house they were told that he had left on his motorbike some weeks ago and hadn't been seen since. Efforts to trace him at first drew a blank. Then Superintendent Osborne decided on a hunch to check the Kenwyn caravan park on the outskirts of Truro, where caravans could sometimes be rented.

A middle-aged woman standing in the doorway of one of the trailers said that a young man staying at the caravan just across from her had a motorbike. She complained that he and his friend drove up at all hours of the night, waking her up.

Three teenage girls occupied the caravan where the biker was staying. The woman said: "These two boys on a motorbike turned up one night. They just moved in with the girls and they've been staying there ever since."

"When was the last time these boys came in late and woke you up?" Superintendent Osborne asked.

"Wednesday night, or rather, early on Thursday morning. I'd just dropped off to sleep at two o'clock when they drove up, their engine roaring. I was furious…"

The Yard detectives walked across to the caravan opposite. A young blonde opened the door.

"Russell Pascoe?" she said in answer to their inquiry. "No, I'm sorry he's not here. He went off on his motorbike an hour ago to see a friend in Constantine."

"Then is his friend here?" Superintendent Osborne asked. "Let me see, what's his name?"

"You mean Dennis Whitty. He's not here either. He said he was going down to the pub."

The detectives thanked the girl and left. Superintendent Osborne put through a call to the temporary office he had established in Constantine, telling officers there to find Pascoe's motorbike and to bring Pascoe in. Then, with the help of a Truro policeman, they found Dennis Whitty at a local pub and took him to Constantine. By the time he was brought to police headquarters Pascoe had been found, and was waiting for him there.

Both suspects were well built and good-looking. Pascoe was 23, Whitty 22, and both were labourers. Interviewed separately, they both denied having gone to Nanjarrow farm on Wednesday night. They had been to a cinema in Truro, they said. But neither could recall the film, and it was soon clear that they were lying.

It was Russell Pascoe who first admitted that they had gone to William Rowe's farm intending to rob him. Whitty had pretended to be a helicopter pilot and he himself had posed as his passenger, in order to gain entry to the house.

"We planned to frighten him into telling us where the money was, but things went wrong," Pascoe said. "So I hit him over the head with a small iron bar. I meant to knock him out, that's all. Dennis took the iron bar from me and went for him.

"I had to walk away, honest I did. I went inside and found four pounds under a piano. Dennis took a watch and two big boxes of matches and some keys from the old man's pockets. We shared the four pounds – two pounds each. I've spent mine.

"I didn't kill him. That was my mate. He went mad, he did. I was afraid to stop him or he would stick me. I had to walk away. I couldn't stop him. He said he'd finished him when he stuck the knife in his throat. I only knocked him over the head with a bar. I just knocked him out.

"When I did, I told Dennis that was enough, but he went mad with the knife. Then he took the bar off me and kept thumping him on the head. He was mad. If I had tried to stop him he would have stuck me."

It emerged that Pascoe spent his childhood at his parents' home only a mile and a half away from Nanjarrow Farm, where he did occasional work as a teenager. During that time the farm was burgled while William Rowe was absent, and now Pascoe admitted being one of the two thieves responsible.

Told of his accomplice's confessions, Whitty said: "I didn't intend to harm the old man, but Pascoe made me stick him with my knife. I stuck him in the chest a couple of times. Then Pascoe was going to hit me, so I stuck him in the neck. We are both over 21, so I suppose we can hang. I was going to give myself up if I hadn't been brought in."

In a subsequent written statement Whitty claimed

that going to rob the farmer was Pascoe's idea. "I didn't mean to go, but he made me. I knocked, and the old man came to the door with a lantern. I told him I'd trouble with the helicopter and asked the old man to show me the phone. Russell hit him on the head with an iron bar. He fell down and Russell kept hitting him. Russell said, 'Go on, stick him.'

"I didn't want to, and I started crying. He told me he would use the bar on me if I didn't do it, so I struck him in the chest three or four times and once in the throat."

Confirming Pascoe's statement that the murder had netted them only £4, he said: "We were after the big money we knew he had hidden in the house. We tore the place apart, searched everywhere, but we couldn't find another penny."

Had they understood William Rowe's document in Esperanto they might have located a fortune, but at about 1 a.m. they abandoned their search. They intended to make a better job of hiding their victim's body, but it proved too heavy to drag further so they dumped it in the outhouse. On the way home they threw the iron bar and the knife into a roadside reservoir. The police later recovered both weapons.

The stolen matches were found in the caravan, and William Rowe's watch was found in the pocket of a raincoat that Whitty kept at Truro gasworks, where he was employed.

Further inquiries revealed that Pascoe left his wife a month earlier and went to live in the caravan with Whitty and the three girls, all aged 19. The five shared two beds, and two of the girls had accompanied Whitty on housebreaking expeditions.

All three girls turned out to know a good deal more about the murder than was at first suspected. The men had asked them for two pairs of nylon stockings to wear over their faces, saying they were going "to do a job" but not saying what it was. They also borrowed gloves, a black jumper and a double-breasted blazer with silver buttons, which Whitty imagined looked like a naval uniform – such as might be worn by a helicopter pilot.

One of the girls told the investigators that when the men returned in the early hours of August 15th Whitty was grinning but Pascoe looked downcast. He said, "We didn't get nothing," and he wiped some blood from Whitty's face. Whitty told his girl friend that there was an incident involving a farmer, and after breakfast he and Pascoe went off to work as usual.

Pascoe's girl friend said she later saw an evening newspaper report of the discovery of William Rowe's body. Showing Whitty the paper, she said to him, "You went to Constantine. Did you do that?"

Whitty replied: "Yes, I did."

The girl told detectives that Pascoe then warned them that if they talked they would share the same fate as William Rowe. One of the two men – she couldn't recall which one – said the farmer was killed because he recognised them.

The full, horrific extent of the elderly farmer's injuries was revealed when Pascoe and Witty appeared before Falmouth magistrates, charged with the murder. The court was told that within 30 seconds William Rowe's skull was shattered. Additionally, he received half-a-dozen scalp wounds, his jaw was broken and his five stab wounds in the chest included one that was five inches deep, which penetrated his heart. He lost part of a finger as he tried to defend himself.

"This murder was premeditated," said Mr. John Woods, prosecuting, "insofar as both men agreed that they were going out for the purpose of theft. They rehearsed with the nylon stockings, but didn't actually wear them. They intended seriously to hurt anyone they encountered. That was the purpose of the helicopter story. It was a cold-blooded and ruthless murder in the furtherance of gain."

The two defendants were committed for trial at Bodmin Assizes. Both pleaded not guilty when they appeared before Mr. Justice Thesiger on October 29th, 1963.

Pascoe's defence counsel, Mr. James Comyn, told the

court that his client had "a discreditable story" to tell, but there was never one single instance when he was trapped. "It is my submission that he told his story well and told it truthfully."

Mr. Norman Skelhorn QC, defending Whitty, said his client was pressurised to take part in the robbery at Nanjarrow Farm, Pascoe telling him: "You will have to come. If you don't, I will scar you for life."

Seeking a verdict of manslaughter on the grounds of diminished responsibility, Mr. Skelhorn said Whitty was afflicted by a hysterical condition and had suffered at least half-a-dozen blackouts. Pascoe's claims that his partner had gone "mad with the knife" supported the picture of a man not in control of his actions.

Whitty himself told the court of "strange and unnatural" experiences in which pictures on the wall changed places overnight and doors opened of their own accord. Saying that he believed in ghosts, he testified: "At four o'clock one morning I saw a figure with wings in the sky as I walked down to the beach."

Pascoe testified that he struck William Rowe on the head, "but not very hard," as the old man stood at the door. He said the farmer fell to his knees and then looked up and asked, "Why did you do that?" Whitty then killed Rowe because he thought their victim might have recognised his companion as the young man who once worked for him.

Summing-up, the judge said it was for the jury to decide on Whitty's mental condition. "What appears to me to be important," Mr. Justice Thesiger continued, "is that this man's particular hysterical attacks are manifested in blackouts and unconsciousness. The result of his attacks of mental abnormality are the fits of unconsciousness. On the night in question there is no evidence of such a fit or blackout."

After retiring for four and a half hours on November 2nd, 1963, the jury found both men guilty of William Rowe's murder and they were sentenced to death.

Although there was little public sympathy for the two killers, the National Campaign for the Abolition of Capital Punishment used the impending executions to press for an end to the death penalty. Placards proclaimed: "On Tuesday December 16th the Home Secretary will murder Whitty and Pascoe."

They got the date wrong. December 16th was a Monday, and it wasn't until the afternoon of Tuesday, December 17th, that Harry Allen checked in at Bristol Prison with his assistant Royston Rickard, ready to hang Russell Pascoe the next morning. At the same time as Pascoe stepped on to the scaffold, Dennis Whitty was hanged at Winchester, executed by Robert Stewart, assisted by Harry Robinson.

An interesting insight into Harry Allen's methods was observed by Robert Douglas, one of the warders in the Pascoe death cell, who wrote a book, *At Her Majesty's Pleasure*, about his experiences. Douglas describes how he and the other warder on duty, named Ken, spent the last night with Russell Pascoe.

"The inner door opens and the Governor enters, accompanied by another man. The three of us stand up.

"'All correct, sir,' Ken states.

"'Thank you.' The Governor smiles and turns to Russell. 'How are you, Pascoe?'

"'All right, sir.'

"The man with the Governor suddenly steps forward towards Russell and sticks his hand out.

"'How do you do, son?" Russell's automatic reaction is to take it. They shake hands.

"'I'm not so bad,' he murmurs. I glance at Ken.

"'Right! We'll be going now,' says the Governor. Immediately he and the man turn on their heels and leave. Russell sits quietly for a moment, then says, 'Who were that with the Governor?'

"I know. I've just had supper with him and his assistant in the officers' mess.

"'Ahhh, I'm not very sure,' mumbles Ken.

"'I bloody knows,' says Russell. 'That were the f------ hangman, weren't it? '"

When the two warders finally agree that the prisoner

has guessed correctly, Russell Pascoe demands to know why the hangman wants to shake hands with him.

"'It's just a thing Pierrepoint always did,' I say, 'and Harry Allen has carried it on. They always come in with the Governor and just stick their hand out.'

"'If I caught on quicker who the bugger was I wouldn't have took 'is hand. F---er! Caught me on the hop, he did.'"

Future historians may puzzle over why it was that despite their horrific, cold-blooded murder of an old, defenceless man, the case of Pascoe and Whitty did nothing to halt the onset of abolition. Russell Pascoe was to be Harry's penultimate hanging. His next appointment on the scaffold would be with the last man to be hanged in Britain.

CHAPTER 11

THE LAST MEN TO HANG

It wasn't much of a night out, but it made a change, and Mrs. Mary Allen (no relation to Harry) had nothing else to do. So when her husband said he and a friend were going to drive from Preston up to Workington in Cumberland to borrow some money, she went along for the ride with her two little children.

She had no idea she was going on a car ride that would end in murder.

In fact, Mary was asleep in the car when, in the early hours of April 7th, 1964, they drew up in King's Avenue, in the Workington suburb of Seaton. Her two children were also sleeping, and none of them woke up when her husband and his friend quietly got out of the car and went to one of the houses in the darkened cul-de-sac.

Three hours later mayhem reigned in King's Avenue. Although it was still only 4 a.m., lights were on in most of the houses and the street was swarming with police officers.

Earlier that night, just before they went to bed around 11 o'clock, King's Avenue residents Joseph Fawcett and his wife had noticed that the living-room light was still on next door, the home of Alan "Jack" West, a 53-year-old bachelor who lived alone and worked at the local laundry. There was nothing untoward in that – Jack West wasn't in the habit of going to bed early.

The Fawcetts were asleep before midnight. At 3 a.m., however, they were awakened by loud thuds from next door. These were followed by lighter thuds. Intrigued, Joseph Fawcett got out of bed, peered through the window, and saw his neighbour's light reflected on windows of the house opposite. Then he heard a car start, and saw it speed away down the road towards

Coronation Avenue, the main road to Seaton town centre.

Feeling that something was amiss, the Fawcetts dressed quickly and went round to Jack West's house. They banged on the front and back doors, but there was no response. Joseph Fawcett then went across the road, roused Walter Lister, who lived in the house opposite, and he phoned the police.

PC Clarke arrived within minutes, and Mrs. Fawcett recalled that Jack West kept a spare front-door key in his garage. She fetched it, and the officer let himself into the house.

The body of Jack West lay at the bottom of the stairs near the front door. The body and the stair carpet were heavily bloodstained – in fact, there was blood on the stairs from top to bottom. A length of metal tubing encased in rubber and half wrapped in a pair of pyjama trousers was lying on the living-room floor. PC Clarke radioed for assistance, and by 4 a.m. the cul-de-sac was teeming with officers.

The Carlisle pathologist arrived as dawn was breaking and he had the body removed for a post-mortem. His examination revealed that the middle-aged bachelor had suffered multiple head injuries and died from a stab wound to the heart.

Detective Inspector Leslie Gibson, in charge of the investigation, had only the cosh and a fingerprint, which wasn't West's, as clues. A search of the house and garden failed to reveal the knife that delivered the fatal blow.

The next clue didn't emerge until lunchtime, when a raincoat that didn't belong to Jack West was found in his bedroom. There was a key-wallet containing a key and a gold medallion inscribed "G. O. Evans, July, 1961," in one of the pockets. There was also a scrap of paper with the name Norma O'Brien and an address scribbled on it.

Miss O'Brien turned out to be a 17-year-old Liverpool factory worker. Shown the medallion, she said she had seen it around the neck of Gwynne Evans, a man she met at her sister's home in 1963. He was known as

Sandy, and she went out with him once or twice. She remembered he lodged with a friend, Peter Allen, in Clarendon Street, Preston.

Meanwhile, in Ormskirk, 18 miles south of Preston, police found an abandoned car. Its Preston owner, James Cook, had reported it stolen, and it bore the fingerprints of two men known to the police. They were Peter Anthony Allen, 21, and Gwynne Owen Evans, 24.

On Wednesday, April 8th, Peter Allen was interviewed by Preston detectives and afterwards taken to Workington police station at 6.45 p.m. Two hours earlier, Detective Sergeant Hodgson questioned Allen's wife Mary in Manchester. Gwynne Evans was with her at the time, and he was arrested on suspicion of murder.

A driving licence bearing the name David Cook was found in one of Evans's pockets, together with a gold wristwatch inscribed with the name J. A. West. "I bought the watch this morning from a man in Preston," Evans said. "I gave him two pounds for it because he wanted some money for petrol."

"But this watch belonged to a man who has just been found murdered," the detective pointed out.

Evans immediately changed his story. "Jack West has been a friend of mine for the last five years," he said. "He told me that if ever I was short of money he would lend me a couple of quid. I will tell you all about it."

Evans then made a statement in which he said he went to Seaton with Peter and Mary Allen and their two children. They arrived in the early hours of the morning and found Jack still up.

"I knocked on the door and Jack came down and let me in," Evans went on. "We were talking inside when there was a knock at the door. Jack went to answer it, and when I followed I saw Peter Allen hitting him with something. I shouted, 'For Christ's sake stop it!' and Peter said, 'He's got the cash and I want it.'"

Evans then described the return journey south. He said he drove out of Seaton at almost 75 miles an hour, and Mary Allen implored him to slow down for the sake of the children. When they got back to Allen's home, he watched Allen burn his bloodstained shirt in the fire grate, and then they all went to Liverpool with West's bank books and drew £10 from the account.

Evans signed his statement and was taken to Workington police station, where Peter Allen was already being questioned by Detective Chief Superintendent William Roberts, while Detective Chief Inspector John Watson made notes. The interview began with Roberts asking Allen when he last worked.

"I've not worked for about a week," Allen replied. "Last Saturday was the last time."

"Where were you yesterday, Tuesday?"

"Liverpool."

"Just describe your movements."

"We left Preston at about 8 a.m. and went by train to Liverpool – me, the wife, two children and my mate Sandy Evans who lodges with us."

"Why did you go?"

"We went to look at empty houses because we'd had notice to quit. We are about ten or fifteen pounds behind with the rent – the wife can tell you."

"Doesn't Sandy give you something?"

"Sandy hasn't been working either."

"You have been brought here because I want to ask you some questions about a man called West who was killed at his home in King's Avenue, Seaton, during the early hours of Tuesday morning."

"You don't mean that man who was murdered? Listen, you can get a stack of Bibles in here and I'll stand on them and swear I know nothing about it."

"Have you been to Workington before today?"

"No."

"Weren't you in Workington about six weeks ago?"

"Yes, I'd forgotten. Sandy brought me and the wife and the youngsters up."

"Where did you go after leaving Liverpool?"

"To New Brighton, and then Seacombe. We couldn't find any houses, so we went down Faulkland Road – that's the place for flats – but they are all coming down.

We left about four-thirty p.m. and got back to Preston between six-thirty and six-forty-five p.m."

"Where did you get the money to go?"

"Sandy got his national assistance."

"Where were you on Monday night?" [This was the night of the murder].

"All Monday night I stayed in – me, the wife, two babies and Sandy. We went to bed about nine-thirty to ten."

"Did Sandy knock about with anyone else besides you and your wife?"

"He didn't knock about with my wife."

"You have been telling me how he went out with you and your wife – did he go out with anyone else?"

"I don't know. I don't think so."

"Would it surprise you to know that they were together in Manchester when the police traced them?"

"It would, very much."

"Well, they were. They are on their way here now. How long have you been wearing those clothes?"

Peter Allen looked down at his trousers. "Two days," he replied.

"Were you wearing them on Monday night?"

"Yes."

"Can you drive?"

"No. I have no licence and I can't drive anyway."

"So if you go out in a car, Sandy drives?"

"Yes."

"Did Sandy have a car on Monday night?"

"Not to my knowledge."

By now Allen was visibly sweating. He was asked: "You weren't in a car on Monday night?"

"No, I wasn't," he replied, taking a cigarette from a packet on the table in front of him. "Can I have a match, please?"

"Whether you are involved in this business or not I don't know," Roberts continued, "but further inquiries will be made, and I'm going to question your wife and Evans when they arrive."

Suddenly, Allen thumped the table with his fist and

buried his face in his arm. "That's lies," he half cried. "All right, I'll tell you. I'd like to tell the whole flipping world about it."

Roberts immediately cautioned him, and then Allen went on, nodding towards Detective Inspector John Watson: "He can tear up what he's written up to now. I'll tell you what happened. It started off as an innocent robbery. Monday night at about nine-thirty we went to a garage in Preston and pinched a car. I picked the wife and babies up, but she didn't know what was going on. We came up here, and when we got here Sandy went in.

"We got there at one-ten. The bloke knew Sandy, and Sandy said he had money lying around. We parked the car in front of the road works. He went in and came out for me about ten to three, and I went in. Sandy told him that he wanted some fresh air and let me in without the chap knowing, but when he came down the stairs he saw me, so I hit him. Sandy had the bar and he gave it to me.

"Sandy put the light out and I was hitting out blindly. I only had my fists until Sandy gave me the bar. I only hit him twice with it, and then I gave it back to Sandy. I went upstairs to see if there was any loose cash, but there wasn't. There was a bunch of letters and two bankbooks in the drawer, and I just grabbed the lot.

"The wife and children were asleep in the car. We went straight down the road towards Cockermouth. I threw my gloves out of the window. When we got to Windermere we ran out of petrol, but Sandy got some. We went to Kendal and the wife cashed her family allowance and we went straight to Liverpool to see my mum.

"On the way back we left the car in a yard, a builder's yard near the bus depot. We got a bus back. Yesterday Sandy got two five-pound notes from a bank in Liverpool. The wife went to the door with him. When we got back I scrubbed my jeans and burned the letters. Sandy took the chap's watch and jacket, and he left his own coat in the house.

"I'll tell you this – I'm glad you've found me. Sandy said it was an easy touch. Who am I to take a human life in my hands? All I wanted was a hundred pounds for a deposit on a house."

"Were you wearing that clothing on Monday night?" Roberts asked.

"No. I burned my shirt and I've washed my jeans. They are at the house. The wife took my jacket with her to Manchester."

"What about shoes? Were you wearing those?"

"Yes, I had these on."

Allen then wrote out his statement. He said: "I was told that it was an easy touch and there would be no violence by my mate G. O. Evans. It all started when I had £44 rates to find, also the sum of £15 and £20 for a fine and arrears on my house. G. O. Evans and I pinched a car from Preston on Monday to go up to Cumberland and attempt to break into J. A. West's house to get some money."

When Mr. West appeared on the stairs, the statement continued, "he made a lunge at me and I panicked. I hit him in the face with my fist and he fell."

The statement went on: "The next thing I remember was seeing Gwynne hit him with a rubber hose pipe. Mr. West then fell downstairs. I went back upstairs to see if I could find any money, leaving Gwynne downstairs." After taking the bankbooks and letters from the bedroom he went back to Gwynne Evans and told him to hurry up. They left the murder scene at 3.15 a.m.

Allen had not mentioned a stab wound or a knife, and neither had the detectives, who now went to another room to interview Evans. First, Roberts asked him if Evans was his real name.

"No," Evans replied, "but I adopted it after I found out that I was born in Innsbruck in 1940, and that both my parents are German."

Told that the detectives were investigating West's death, Evans said: "Yes, sir, I know. I'll tell you everything that happened. We set out to see my mother by car at about ten-thirty on Monday night. I decided to steal a car and take Peter, his wife and children with me. My mother has a wristwatch belonging to me that I could sell for some money.

"I've known Mr. West for some time and he had said to me that if ever I was in Workington and required money, to see him. I was going to ask him for the loan of a hundred pounds. We got there about 2 a.m. I knocked on the door and he said, 'I didn't expect to see you tonight.'

"I told him I was up to see my mother. He asked me where I was staying and I said I had a friend with me in the car. He asked me to go to bed with him. I don't know whether anyone knows it or not, but West was a homosexual.

"A knock came to the door and West said, 'Who can that be?' I said I didn't know. He went to the door and Peter rushed him and said, 'I want some bloody money.' I said, 'Well, leave him alone, he hasn't got anything.'

"When I went up to the bedroom, Jack said he wanted something from the airing cupboard and I put my coat on the chair. Then he said it didn't matter. I don't know anything about a knife. I don't have to use a knife to kill a man – I'm an expert at judo and karate. I never hit Jack – it was Peter that did all the hitting.

"Me and Peter got the bank books from a cupboard in the kitchen, and I picked the watch up from the kitchen table. I got a jacket from the kitchen as well, because Peter said he wanted one. Mary knew I was going to borrow money, but she must have known what happened because Peter was covered in blood. I had no blood on me – I was wearing these clothes.

"We set off in the car and Peter threw a pair of gloves and some other object out of the window. I think we were just outside Windermere. We stopped at Kendal to get Mary's family allowance. Then we went to Liverpool and I got ten pounds on the bank books. Peter told me to do it, and he said he would then go into another bank and get another ten pounds, but he didn't.

"We went to Wallasey and New Brighton. Then back

through Ormskirk, where we left the car at about 7.30 and got a bus back to Preston. At Clarendon Street [their home in Preston] Peter burned his shirt and tore the bank books and burned them. He poured lighter fuel over his shirt. He also burned some letters.

"This morning Mary and I went to see Mary's mother in Manchester, but more than anything else to borrow a hundred pounds to put down on a house. I went to see my girl in Manchester, and then I went to collect Mary at her mother's. The police picked me up there. They found Jack West's watch in my pocket.

"Peter told his wife to take his jacket to Manchester and lose it. She said, 'Burn it?' but he said, 'No, take it on to Manchester and get rid of it.' Peter washed his jeans and tried to wash the bloodstains from his jacket."

Evans concluded: "Jack West was just like my own father." But significantly, his reference to a knife was unprompted. The police had made no mention of it.

Evans then wrote a statement in which he said that Jack West had refused to offer him a loan. "I thought he would have given me a cheque, but he just said, "I'll see." The statement said, "I knew Peter always carried a knife in his pocket or in his belt. He has told me he used a knife on a man in Manchester. On this night I did not see his knife because he had it stuck down the inside of his trousers. He must have thrown it away with his gloves.

"Although I did intend robbing Jack West I did not intend using violence. The killing was all Peter's fault. I never once hit him."

Parts of Evans's account were perhaps true. After he entered the house alone he may have had some kind of sex with West, and that was why he left his raincoat in the bedroom. It may also be why West was undressed and the cosh was found wrapped in the pyjama trousers. And Evans was in the house alone with West for at least an hour before Allen, evidently tiring of waiting outside in the car, burst in.

Both men were charged with capital murder in the

furtherance of theft, which they denied when their trial began at Manchester Crown Court on June 19th, 1964.

Outlining the case for the prosecution, Mr. J. D. Cantley QC said the stolen car was seen in Windermere shortly after the murder. The fingerprints of both the accused were found in it, and a knife was found in undergrowth bordering a road in Windermere. "That knife was stained with blood," said Mr. Cantley, "and the blood group was 'A,' Mr. West's group. The two prisoners are both group 'O.'"

The prosecutor read out the statements made by Allen and Evans, each blaming the other. A director of the Lakeland Laundry, Robert Holliday, told the court that Jack West had been employed as a van driver for about 35 years, and in 1954 he was presented with a watch in recognition of 25 years' service. The watch was inscribed with his name and date of presentation. Mr. Holliday identified it as the one found in Evans's possession.

The pathologist told the jury that West received a chest wound three-and-a-half inches deep, which penetrated his heart. He also had multiple head wounds, including fractures of the bone between his right eye and ear, and the bone at the base of his nose, extending to his jawbone.

Norma O'Brien, who gave the police Allen's address, identified the raincoat and medallion found at Mr. West's home, saying she recognised them as belonging to Evans.

On the fourth day of the trial Peter Allen went into the witness-box. He said he first met Evans in November, 1963. Evans had previously worked with Mr. West, and they decided to visit him to obtain money. "If West was out," Allen continued, "we were to break in. I made the point clear to Evans that there was to be no violence, and he said, 'All right.'"

When he went to join Evans inside the house, Evans was going upstairs. "I saw an object sticking out of his pocket. It looked just like a short bar. I had never seen it before. As I neared the top of the stairs, Evans turned to the bathroom. I continued up the stairs and when I got to the bend West came out of a room on to the landing."

Allen was asked by his counsel, Mr. S. G. Nance, if he could say how West was dressed. "He had some clothes on, but I could not say what they were," he replied.

Mr. Justice Ashworth said that when West was found he was naked from the waist down. Was he like that when Allen saw him?

Allen said he could not remember. He went on: "Mr. West said to me words to the effect, 'Who the bloody hell are you?' When I didn't answer he made a lunge at me. I panicked, drew back my fist and hit him. The lights then went out and the next thing I can remember is seeing Evans hitting West with this bar effort.

"Evans put the bar in my hand and I took a swipe at West once or twice. Then he fell down the stairs. I gave the bar back to Evans and he hit him a few more times with the bar and he toppled backwards." He and Evans then went into West's bedroom and took bank books and papers from drawers. Then he went downstairs.

"Mr. West was lying at the bottom of the stairs with his head against the wall. He was mumbling a bit. I bent down to pick him up." Asked about the mumblings, Allen said: "I caught, 'Don't hit me no more.'"

He continued: "Evans came out of a room nearly opposite the stairs. He put his hand somewhere inside his coat and pulled out a knife and stuck it in West. I said, 'What the bloody hell did you do that for?' Evans turned to me and said, 'You are all right. Jack wouldn't recognise you, but he recognised me.'"

Allen was cross-examined by Mr. G. W. Guthrie Jones, defending Evans, who suggested that violence was not required to subdue West.

"I was in a panic," Allen replied. "You do a lot of things you don't realise in a panic. You are not thinking straight."

The judge asked: "Would you care to tell the jury why you beat him with a cosh?"

"I don't know, sir," Allen replied. He denied that parts of his story were an invention to save his skin. Asked why he bent down to pick up West, he said, "I was ashamed of what I had done and had come to my senses by then." He denied inventing the story of picking up West in order to explain why his jacket had blood on it.

Evans' defence team seemed to regard Mary Allen as a possible hostile witness. She admitted that she visited Evans' parents' home at Camerton, giving the impression that she was his wife and shared the same bedroom with him, but she denied that they had been lovers. She sent letters to both her husband and Evans in prison, and in a letter to Evans she wrote:

"How could you lie, knowing Peter is taking all the blame, and could possibly hang for the murder? I shall never forgive. All I feel for you now is a deep, bitter hatred. All the lies you have told will do you no good. If you get off it will be on your conscience. I am with Peter all the way."

Gwynne Evans told the court that he had known Peter Allen for about five years. When they set out for West's home, he told Allen that he was prepared to rob, but no violence was to be used. He had seen the length of piping at Allen's house, and the next time he saw it was in the magistrates' court at Warrington. He did not take a knife with him, and he did not know that one was being taken on the trip.

When Allen began hitting West on the stairs he did not intervene, he said, because he panicked. He did not know that West was dead until he read a newspaper the next day. He did not throw away a knife at Windermere, and said he had seen one in a sheath on Allen's belt some five to six weeks earlier.

In his closing speech to the court, Allen's counsel Mr. Nance claimed that his client had told the truth regardless of the consequences, whereas Evans was lying, trying to shift the blame for everything as far away from himself as possible. The prosecution's evidence had not proved Allen guilty of murder or capital murder, Mr. Nance contended.

Mr. Morris Jones, defending Evans, told the jury: "He was not the person who on that occasion used violence, and to that extent he is entitled to a verdict of not guilty of capital murder. The Crown has failed to prove that Evans was a party to the violence that was used. It came from the eruption of Allen in the house."

Summing-up, Mr. Justice Ashworth told the jury: "It would be wholly wrong if you were to say that West was murdered, there were two men there, they must both be guilty. Your verdicts need not be the same for each man, but there is a rider in this case. What each man said to the police is evidence in his case, but it is not evidence against the other man at all. Each man has given evidence before you. When a prisoner comes to give evidence in court and implicates his co-accused, as each man has in this case, then his story will be challenged by counsel for his co-accused."

The judge went on to urge the jury to examine the evidence of Mary Allen with very great care. "It would be wrong for me to say she must be disbelieved. That is your problem, not mine. You may think she has an interest to serve in getting her husband off, and getting Evans convicted. The question of whether she committed adultery is not for you or me. We are not here to investigate that.

"What did you make of Allen? Much slower on the uptake, not such bright, sparkling responses to questions; dull, you might have thought at times.

"What about Evans? Boastful, that is how he is best described. He was seldom at a loss for an answer, and in a sense he did not do himself justice because he answered too quickly. Was he glib, plausible? Maybe, yes. The real decision is, was he truthful?"

Referring to the weapons, the judge said there was little doubt that they both came from the Allens' home in Clarendon Street, and both were used on West. The crucial question was, who used them? One, the other, or both the accused?

On July 7th it took the jury just 45 minutes to decide

that both men were guilty of capital murder, and they were sentenced to death. Seven days later their appeals were dismissed, the Lord Chief Justice, Lord Parker, commenting: "A more brutal murder it would be difficult to imagine."

When Mary Allen visited her husband at Walton Prison, Liverpool, on August 12th, after his reprieve was rejected, he went berserk. He hurled himself against the thick glass separating them, cracking and splintering it, and warders dragged him back to his cell.

Evans was also refused a reprieve, and that same day his mother sent a telegram to the Queen at Balmoral, seeking the royal prerogative of mercy on the grounds of her son's age and his history of mental trouble. His parents had earlier made it known that they were not German, and he was born John Walby, at Maryport in Cumberland.

That night demonstrators against capital punishment held a vigil outside Walton Prison. "No more hangings," said one of their banners. "Why take another life?" asked another. During the night demonstrators handed out leaflets that pointed out that if Allen and Evans had been convicted of killing without stealing, they would not have been sentenced to death. Such a hypothetical technicality, it seemed, was sufficient to obfuscate the horrifically brutal death they handed out to Jack Allen.

About 40 people were outside the prison when Peter Allen was hanged at 8 a.m. on August 13th by Robert Stewart and his assistant Harry Robinson. In his log Robert Stewart recorded that Allen "smashed his head against a wall during his last visit and broke a finger. As I was strapping his wrists in the morning he shouted, 'Jesus!' That was it. Not another word."

But there were no demonstrators at 8 a.m. that same day at Strangeways as Harry Allen and Royston Rickard dispatched Gwynne Evans.

Allen and Evans were the last men to hang in Britain, and Robert Stewart and Harry Allen left Walton and Strangeways that morning never to officiate at another

British execution. More death sentences were passed after 1964, but all the condemned prisoners were reprieved, and capital punishment was abolished in November, 1965.

EPILOGUE

THE END OF THE ROPE

When it was all over, he used to say, he planned to leave England and start a hotel in Spain – a popular idea among sun-starved Brits in the mid-1960s. He had enjoyed organising highly successful charter trips for his pub customers but took on board their continuous complaints about "the oily food." He thought a Lancashire hotel – "you know, a real home from home with plain food" – would make a lot of money. The idea came to nothing, which was probably just as well. Harry and Doris retired to Fleetwood in Lancashire – a long way from sunny Spain.

So, while MPs were finally deciding against hanging, the country's chief executioner was out shooting on the Pennine moors above his home. When he came back with a brace of pheasants it was to discover that he was more or less out of a job.

The news did not please him. He was a fervent supporter of capital punishment. "Hanging should never have been abolished," he said. "Regardless of what anyone says, it's a deterrent. It's also a perfect system of execution because it's painless." Abolitionists, he went on, "make my blood boil. All this sympathy for people who commit murder amazes me.

"It is not a question of malice or revenge. It's just that there has to be something to stop people going too far, and what greater deterrent can there be than the threat of losing your own life? There is no doubt in my mind – the rope ought to come back."

Most of all, he said, it should come back for acts of terrorism. "You get annoyed when you read about terrorist murders. You think, what a damn shame. You don't like to see innocent people slaughtered. It's not murder any more, it's public slaughter."

As he grew older, Harry moved from the Woodman

Inn to a club in Blackburn and finally to the cottage in Fleetwood. But he was always ready to hold court in retirement. For a public servant – he was still the official hangman – he was as outspoken as ever. "The country needs a hangman to deter this unending spate of murders which have occurred since the death penalty was abolished.

"It's terrible that today judges pass sentences of imprisonment for life when they must feel in their hearts that the only real penalty, the only true justice, would be the death penalty.

"There are some people that society would be well rid of. All crimes of violence – the killing of policemen, children, murder for gain and for lust – should be paid for with the death penalty. I am a Christian, and I feel there is great truth in the teaching of the Bible – an eye for an eye and a tooth for a tooth."

He didn't think there was anything barbaric about hanging. "I have studied the other methods and our way is best. It is quick and humane." He was asked, if hanging were to be re-introduced for murder after a long lay-off, would he have lost his skill? No, he riposted. "It's just like riding a bike. Once you've learned you never forget."

Visitors who came to see him while the parliamentary debate on abolition was taking place were surprised not to see a sinister figure as the white-haired grandfather strode in from the Lancashire fields, shedding his sheepskin coat. They found him humorous and direct, almost paternal, as he puffed a bit from the exertion and the frost.

Walking the moors – often seven miles a morning – in search of pheasant, partridge, rabbits or foxes was the way he kept in trim. He hated the idea of doing press-ups or similar gymnastics.

He punctuated his retirement with spells as a factory security officer, and for that he felt he had to keep fit. He didn't like the word redundant applied to his job, and because he held his official executioner position and theoretically could be called at any time to hang someone, he would never consider himself redundant. In fact, after hanging was abolished one working scaffold was still kept in Britain – at Wandsworth Prison.

Every year the postman brought thousands of letters to Harry's cottage in Fleetwood, Lancashire, almost all in support of hanging. Perhaps his memory began to rust with age, because he couldn't remember the number of people he hanged. He thought it ran into hundreds, which of course was an over-estimate. Nor could he remember much about the last execution. "It was in Manchester – I think, of two men who murdered a farmer. I used to keep a record in a book but I destroyed it after I found my little girl reading it one day. I realised that it wasn't the right thing to do. I've always kept quiet about my job, but I've always thought it to be very necessary.

""It would be a lovely thing if there were no more murders," he said. "In that case I'd be happy to be redundant. But I don't think that will happen. When I get up in the morning I see that the world is a lot worse than it was and that nowadays murders are so commonplace that they only rate about four lines in the paper. Somehow the murders seem more callous and more wicked than ever these days."

After capital punishment for murder was abolished in Britain in November, 1965, it continued to be available in law – although obviously unused – in Northern Ireland, the Irish Republic, the Channel Islands and the Isle of Man, and Harry continued to receive requests for his services from these countries.

So Harry quite rightly maintained until his death that so far as Britain was concerned he never officially retired because, after the death penalty was abolished for murder, it was still available under English and Scottish law for high treason, piracy with violence and arson in a royal dockyard. This last offence was abolished in 1971, and in 1998, six years after Harry died, it was abolished for the other two offences, making the United Kingdom finally abolitionist for all offences in peace and war.

In all, Harry executed or helped to execute 82

convicted murderers in Britain and Ireland, and when he gave up hanging he relaxed, gave interviews and began to talk. What was always striking was his zealous defence of capital punishment at a time when Parliament and the liberals had turned their backs on it.

"This argument that it's morally wrong to execute a fellow human being is all wrong," he said in an interview when he was 71. "Men and women who commit wilful, premeditated murders have forfeited their right to live." And he added: "I would urge all those MPs considering whether to restore capital punishment for murder to reflect the views of the vast majority of the electorate.

"The people of Britain are aware that since the death penalty for murder was abolished, crimes of violence, armed robberies and horrific killings have escalated. It's obvious to the man in the street that the ultimate deterrent would reverse this frightening trend.

"I don't believe that crimes of passion, where, for instance, a husband finds his wife in bed with another bloke, should be punishable by death. No penalty will ever prevent those sorts of killings. But I'm sure that armed robbers would think twice about using loaded weapons if they faced the prospect of being topped."

This view was repeated again long after his retirement, when he said in a newspaper interview: "If anyone is guilty of wilful, premeditated murder, he or she deserves to die."

He went on: "The world would be a safer place if people like Moors murderers Ian Brady and Myra Hindley, or Yorkshire Ripper Peter Sutcliffe had been customers of mine. Is it any more humane to cage them for life? Would women or children be safe if they were released?

"And what if they escaped? No prison is 100 per cent safe. I'm completely convinced that everyone I executed was guilty."

Harry always demonstrated an immense pride in his role as Britain's chief executioner, and he wasn't above a bit of hyperbole when he talked about it. "There is no shortage of people wanting to take over from me," he once said. "There are thousands of applications a day – I'll bet the number of people on the waiting list would stretch from here to Manchester."

He had had "dozens of apprentices" to train, but none of them came up to his requirements. "When the time came for them to watch their first actual hanging, they went in at the knees. Even the toughest among them wasn't able to go through with it.

"It isn't that I'm a cruel man, or that I lack compassion. It's just that I regard the job as a job that I do to the best of my ability. If you have a hanging law, there has to be someone capable of performing the service of public executioner. I am capable. That's all there is to it."

It was probably because of his dedication that he echoed Doris's disappointment with his treatment by the Home Office when the job was over and done with. "I would have thought that after working for the Government for so long, I would have had some letter of acknowledgement of my services," he said.

Harry Allen died on August 14th, 1992, just one month after the last-ever death sentence was passed in the British Isles – in the Isle of Man. The date, July 10th, 1992, was also the day that Albert Pierrepoint died.

APPENDIX

THE HANGINGS OF HARRY ALLEN

Compiled by Matthew Spicer

Locations
Harry Allen took part in the execution of 82 murderers (including one woman) between 1941 and 1964. He worked at the following prisons:

Prison	No. of hangings	Prison	No. of hangings
Aberdeen	1	Leeds [Armley]	9
Bedford	2	Lincoln	4
Belfast	2	Liverpool [Walton]	4
Birmingham [Winson Green]	6	Manchester [Strangeways]	5
Bristol	3	Norwich	2
Cardiff	1	Pentonville	16
Durham	5	Shrewsbury	2
Edinburgh [Saughton]	1	St. Helier [Newgate Street]	1
Glasgow [Barlinnie]	2	Wandsworth	13
Holloway	1	Winchester	2

That makes 74 in England, four in Scotland, two in Northern Ireland and one each in Wales and Jersey.

"Culprits"
The youngest person Harry hanged was an 18-year-old in 1960; including this one, he was party to the execution of 11 people under the age of 21; 27 aged between 21 and 24; 10 between 25 and 29; 23 in their 30s; 10 in their 40s. The oldest person Harry hanged was a 53-year-old in 1954.

Assisting – and being assisted
Of his 53 jobs as an assistant, Harry worked with Albert Pierrepoint 40 times and Steve Wade nine times. Wade was also present at the hanging of the five German POWs following Harry's "comeback" in 1945. Harry also assisted Albert Pierrepoint's uncle Tom four times.

The men who worked with Harry were:

Assistant	No. of times assisted
Thomas Cunliffe	2
Samuel Plant	6
Royston Rickard	10
Harry Robinson	3
Harry Smith	4
Robert Stewart	1
John Underhill	3

Thomas Cunliffe came from Greater Manchester and joined the Official List in 1956 but was sacked in 1959 after four executions.

Samuel Plant came from the south-east of England and joined the list in 1960. He had carried out six executions when capital punishment for murder was abolished in November, 1965. He died in 2002.

Royston Rickard also came from the south-east of England and joined the list in 1953, assisting in 17 hangings up to 1965. He died in 1999.

Harry Robinson came from the west Midlands and joined the list at the same time as Thomas Cunliffe. He assisted at seven executions up to 1965 and died in 2006.

Harry Smith came from south Yorkshire and joined the list in 1950. He assisted at 23 jobs, the last being in 1959.

Robert Stewart, a Scot, was the only man to work with Harry as an assistant who was himself an actual executioner, and he was also present with Harry at a double hanging in 1951. He joined the list with Harry Smith and became an actual executioner in March 1956. However, due to the restrictions of the death penalty under the Homicide Act (1957) he only carried out six jobs as "number one," including the simultaneous final one in 1964. Including the jobs with Harry he did 26 as an assistant. He died in South Africa in 1989.

John Underhill joined the list with Samuel Plant and also came from the south-east of England. By the end of hanging, he had assisted at three UK executions. However, he had also worked as an assistant executioner in Singapore during the 1950s.

Notes
Harry worked on two double executions where **Harry Critchell** was also present. Critchell, a Londoner, had joined the list with Steve Wade in 1940, helping on 29 executions until he was sacked in 1948.

At the double execution at Wandsworth in April, 1951 was one **Herbert Allen**, who may have also been known as "Harry" (shown as "HA2" in the table that follows). From the west Midlands, he joined the list in 1949 and assisted at 12 hangings until he was sacked in 1951.

A contemporary and friend of Herbert Allen was **Syd Dernley**, who in the late 1980s and early 1990s became a minor celebrity following the publication of his book *The Hangman's Tale*. Dernley assisted at 23 jobs between 1949 and 1952, before being sacked in 1954. From the east Midlands, he died in 1994 and was, at the time, often incorrectly described as Britain's last surviving hangman. It is quite possible even in 2008 that there are men who were hangmen in this country who are still alive today.

The facts in this statistical overview of Harry Allen's career as hangman are accurate to the best of my knowledge; any additions or corrections may be sent to the publisher for inclusion in future editions of True Detective Magazine.

MCS
2008

THE HANGINGS OF HARRY ALLEN – 1: AS ASSISTANT

Date	Condemned	Place	No. 1	No. 2	Other
Feb 11th, 1941	HOLMES, Clifford	Manchester – Strangeways	TP	HA	
Mar 6th, 1941	WHITE, Henry Lyndo	Durham	TP	HA	
Sep 4th, 1941	SMITH, John	Manchester – Strangeways	TP	HA	
Dec 3rd, 1941	SMITH, John Ernest	Wandsworth	AP	HA	
Oct 6th, 1945	BRUELING, Heinz	Pentonville	AP	HA	SW
Oct 6th, 1945	GOLTZ, Joachim	Pentonville	AP	HA	SW
Oct 6th, 1945	KOENING, Eric Pallme	Pentonville	AP	HA	SW
Oct 6th, 1945	MERTENS, Josef	Pentonville	AP	HA	SW
Oct 6th, 1945	ZUEHLSDORF, Kurst	Pentonville	AP	HA	SW
Jan 8th, 1946	BATTY, William	Leeds – Armley	TP	HA	
Mar 26th, 1946	CHARLES, Arthur	Durham	SW	HA	
Sep 6th, 1946	MASON, David Baillie	Wandsworth	AP	HA	HC
Sep 6th, 1946	SMITH, Sidney John	Wandsworth	AP	HA	HC
Dec 10th, 1946	MATHIESON, John	Pentonville	AP	HA	
Jan 3rd, 1947	SHEMINANT, Stanley	Liverpool – Walton	SW	HA	
Sep 19th, 1947	GERAGHTY, Christopher James	Pentonville	AP	HA	HC
Sep 19th, 1947	JENKINS, Charles Henry	Pentonville	AP	HA	HC
Dec 30th, 1947	JURKIEWICZ, Eugene	Bristol	AP	HA	HC
Feb 19th, 1948	CROSS, Walter John	Pentonville	AP	HA	
Nov 19th, 1948	GRIFFITHS, Peter	Liverpool – Walton	AP	HA	
Dec 30th, 1948	OSBORNE, Arthur George	Leeds – Armley	SW	HA	
Jan 27th, 1949	SEMINI, George	Liverpool – Walton	AP	HA	
Apr 21st, 1949	LEWIS, Harold	Pentonville	AP	HA	
Jun 2nd, 1949	NEVILLE, Dennis	Leeds – Armley	SW	HA	
Jul 28th, 1949	CHAMBERLAIN, Sydney Archibald	Winchester	AP	HA	
Sep 28th, 1949	JONES, William Claude	Pentonville	AP	HA	
Dec 30th, 1949	COUZINS, Ernest Soper	Wandsworth	AP	HA	
Mar 28th, 1950	KELLY, George	Liverpool – Walton	AP	HA	

Date	Name	Prison			
Mar 30th, 1950	SHARPE, Walter	Leeds – Armley	SW	HA	
Aug 16th, 1950	PRICE, Albert	Wandsworth	AP	HA	
Apr 3rd, 1951	WATKINS, William Arthur	Birmingham – Winson Green	AP	HA	
Apr 25th, 1951	BROWN, Joseph	Wandsworth	AP	HA	SD, HA(2)
Apr 25th, 1951	SMITH, Edward Charles	Wandsworth	AP	HA	SD, HA(2)
May 9th, 1951	SHAUGHNESSY, William Edward	Winchester	AP	HA	
Jun 12th, 1951	DAND, John	Manchester – Strangeways	AP	HA	
Jul 19th, 1951	MOORE, Dennis Albert	Norwich	AP	HA	SD, RS
Jul 19th, 1951	REYNOLDS, Alfred George	Norwich	AP	HA	SD, RS
Feb 6th, 1952	MOORE, Alfred	Leeds – Armley	SW	HA	
May 7th, 1952	SINGH, Ajit	Cardiff	AP	HA	
Jul 8th, 1952	HUXLEY, Harold	Shrewsbury	AP	HA	
Oct 9th, 1952	JOHNSON, Peter Cyril	Pentonville	AP	HA	
Dec 24th, 1952	APPLEBY, Herbert	Durham	SW	HA	
Jan 28th, 1953	BENTLEY, Derek William	Wandsworth	AP	HA	
Oct 20th, 1953	GREENAWAY, John Owen	Bristol	AP	HA	
Dec 23rd, 1953	NEWLAND, George James	Pentonville	AP	HA	
Jan 27th, 1954	LUBINA, Wilhelm	Leeds – Armley	SW	HA	
Apr 14th, 1954	DOOHAN, John Reginald	Wandsworth	AP	HA	
Jun 23rd, 1954	ROBERTSON, George Alexander	Edinburgh – Saughton	AP	HA	
Aug 12th, 1954	FOWLER, Harold	Lincoln	AP	HA	
Dec 15th, 1954	CHRISTOPHI, Stylou Pantopiou	Holloway	AP	HA	
May 24th, 1955	ROBINSON, James	Lincoln	AP	HA	
Jul 26th, 1955	CROSS, Frederick Arthur	Birmingham – Winson Green	AP	HA	
Aug 2nd, 1955	ROBERTS, Corbett Montagu	Birmingham – Winson Green	SW	HA	

HA = Harry Allen
HC = Harry Critchell
HS = Harry Smith
JU = John Underhill

TP = Tom Pierrepoint
SD = Syd Dernley
RR = Royston Rickard
SP = Samuel Plant

AP = Albert Pierrepoint
HA(2) = Herbert Allen
TC = Thomas Cunliffe

SW = Steve Wade
RS = Robert Stewart
HR = Harry Robinson

THE HANGINGS OF HARRY ALLEN – 2: AS NUMBER 1

Date	Condemned	Place	No. 1	No. 2
Jul 23rd, 1957	VICKERS, John Willson	Durham	HA	HS
Dec 4th, 1957	HOWARD, Dennis	Birmingham – Winson Green	HA	RR
Jul 11th, 1958	MANUEL, Peter Thomas	Glasgow – Barlinnie	HA	HS
Aug 12th, 1958	KAVANAGH, Matthew	Birmingham – Winson Green	HA	TC
Sep 3rd, 1958	STOKES, Frank	Durham	HA	HS
Feb 10th, 1959	JONES, Ernest Raymond	Leeds – Armley	HA	HS
Apr 28th, 1959	CHRIMES, Joseph	Pentonville	HA	RR
May 8th, 1959	MARWOOD, Ronald Henry	Pentonville	HA	HR
Aug 14th, 1959	WALDEN, Bernard Hugh	Leeds – Armley	HA	TC
Oct 9th, 1959	HUCHET, Francis Joseph	St Helier – Newgate Street	HA	RR
Nov 9th, 1959	PODOLA, Guenther Fritz	Wandsworth	HA	RR
Sep 1st, 1960	CONSTANTINE, John Louis	Lincoln	HA	RR
Nov 10th, 1960	FORSYTH, Frances George	Wandsworth	HA	RR
Dec 22nd, 1960	MILLER, Anthony Joseph	Glasgow – Barlinnie	HA	RS
Jan 27th, 1961	GNYPIUK, Wasyl	Lincoln	HA	JU
Feb 9th, 1961	RILEY, George	Shrewsbury	HA	SP
Mar 29th, 1961	DAY, John	Bedford	HA	HR
May 25th, 1961	TERRY, Victor John	Wandsworth	HA	SP
Jun 29th, 1961	PANKOTAI, Zsiga	Leeds – Armley	HA	HR
Jul 6th, 1961	BUSH, Edwin Albert	Pentonville	HA	JU
Jul 25th, 1961	McLAUGHLIN, Samuel	Belfast	HA	RR
Sep 8th, 1961	NIEMASZ, Hendryck	Wandsworth	HA	SP
Dec 20th, 1961	McGLADDERY, Robert Andrew	Belfast	HA	SP
Apr 4th, 1962	HANRATTY, James	Bedford	HA	RR
Nov 20th, 1962	GREY, Oswald Augustus	Birmingham – Winson Green	HA	SP
Nov 28th, 1962	SMITH, James	Manchester – Strangeways	HA	JU
Aug 15th, 1963	BURNETT, Henry John	Aberdeen	HA	SP
Dec 17th, 1963	PASCOE, Russell	Bristol	HA	RR
Aug 13th, 1964	EVANS, Gwynne Owen	Manchester – Strangeways	HA	RR

Wandsworth Prison Museum

Stewart McLaughlin, author of *Britain's Last Hangman*, is a serving prison officer at London's Wandsworth Prison and is also the curator of the Wandsworth Prison Museum, which opened in 2008. Here he has collected together documents, photographs, furniture, and artefacts related to the prison; the museum is located next door to the prison itself. Stewart is on hand to give historical talks to museum visitors about the prison.

Among the Wandsworth Prison Museum's exhibits are ropes from the prison's gallows

His aim in setting up the museum has been to forge links between the prison and the community, which has had a prison in its borough for more than 150 years.

The museum is now open to members of the public who are advised to write to **The Wandsworth Prison Museum, c/o POA Office, HMP Wandsworth, Heathfield Road, London SW18 3HS** for details of times when the museum is open.